New Perspectives on

MICROSOFT ACCESS® 2000

Brief

JOSEPH J. ADAMSKI
Grand Valley State University

KATHLEEN T. FINNEGAN

COURSE
TECHNOLOGY

Thomson Learning™

ONE MAIN STREET, CAMBRIDGE, MA 02142

Australia • Canada • Denmark • Japan • Mexico • New Zealand • Philippines
Puerto Rico • Singapore • South Africa • Spain • United Kingdom • United States

New Perspectives on Microsoft® Access® 2000 — Brief is published by Course Technology.

Senior Editor	Donna Gridley	Developmental Editor	Jessica Evans
Senior Product Manager	Rachel Crapser	Production Editor	Daphne Barbas
Product Manager	Catherine Donaldson	Text Designer	Meral Dabcovich
Associate Product Manager	Karen Shortill	Cover Art Designer	Douglas Goodman
Editorial Assistant	Melissa Dezotell		

© 1999 by Course Technology, a division of Thomson Learning.

For more information contact:

Course Technology
One Main Street
Cambridge, MA 02142
Or find us on the World Wide Web at: http://www.course.com

Asia (excluding Japan)
Thomson Learning
60 Albert Street, #15-01
Albert Complex
Singapore 189969

Latin America
Thomson Learning
Seneca, 53
Colonia Polanco
11560 Mexico D.F. Mexico

Japan
Thomson Learning
Palaceside Building 5F
1-1-1 Hitotsubashi, Chiyoda-ku
Tokyo 100 0003 Japan

South Africa
Thomson Learning
Zonnebloem Building,
Constantia Square
526 Sixteenth Road
P.O. Box 2459
Halfway House, 1685
South Africa

Australia/New Zealand
Nelson/Thomson Learning
102 Dodds Street
South Melbourne, Victoria 3205

UK/Europe/Middle East
Thomson Learning
Berkshire House
168-173 High Holborn
London
WC1V 7AA United Kingdom

Business Press/Thomson Learning
Berkshire House
168-173 High Holborn
London WC1V 7AA United Kingdom

Thomson Nelson & Sons LTD
Nelson House
Mayfield Road
Walton-on-Thames
KT12 5PL United Kingdom

Canada
Nelson/Thomson Learning
1120 Birchmount Road
Scarborough, Ontario
Canada M1K 5G4

Spain
Paraninfo/Thomson Learning
Calle Magallanes, 25
28015-MADRID
ESPANA

Distrubution Services
Thomson Learning
Ceriton House
North Way
Andover, Hampshire SP10 5BE

International Headquarters
Thomson Learning
International Division
290 Harbor Drive, 2nd Floor
Stamford, CT 06902-7477

Trademarks

Disclaimer

Course Technology reserves the right to revise this publication and make changes from time to time in its content without notice.

ISBN 0-7600-7088-1

Printed in the United States of America

3 4 5 6 7 8 9 10 BM 04 03 02 01

PREFACE

The New Perspectives Series

About New Perspectives

Course Technology's **New Perspectives Series** is an integrated system of instruction that combines text and technology products to teach computer concepts, the Internet, and microcomputer applications. Users consistently praise this series for its innovative pedagogy, use of interactive technology, creativity, accuracy, and a supportive and engaging style.

How is the New Perspectives Series different from other series?

The **New Perspectives Series** distinguishes itself by **innovative technology**, from the renowned Course Labs to the state-of-the-art multimedia that is integrated with our Concepts texts. Other distinguishing features include **sound instructional design, proven pedagogy,** and **consistent quality.** Each tutorial has students learn features in the context of solving a realistic case problem rather than simply learning a laundry list of features. With the **New Perspectives Series,** instructors report that students have a complete, integrative learning experience that stays with them. They credit this high retention and competency to the fact that this series incorporates critical thinking and problem-solving with computer skills mastery. In addition, we work hard to ensure accuracy by using a multi-step quality assurance process during all stages of development. Instructors focus on teaching and students spend more time learning.

What course is this book appropriate for?

New Perspectives on Microsoft® Access® 2000—Brief can be used in any course in which you want students to learn the essential topics of Microsoft Access 2000, including planning, creating, and maintaining a database, and creating reports, queries, and forms. It is particularly recommended for a short course on Access. This book assumes that students have learned basic Windows 95, 98, or NT navigation and file management skills from Course Technology's *New Perspectives on Microsoft Windows 95—Brief,* or the equivalent book for Windows 98 or NT.

Proven Pedagogy

Tutorial Tips Page This page, following the Table of Contents, offers students suggestions on how to effectively plan their study and lab time, what to do when they make a mistake, how to use the Reference Windows, MOUS grids, Quick Checks, and other features of the New Perspectives Series.

Tutorial Case Each tutorial begins with a problem presented in a case that is meaningful to students. The case turns the task of learning how to use an application into a problem-solving process.

45-minute Sessions Each tutorial is divided into sessions that can be completed in about 45 minutes to an hour. Sessions allow instructors to more accurately allocate time in their syllabus, and students to better manage their own study time.

Step-by-Step Methodology We make sure students can differentiate between what they are to *do* and what they are to *read*. Through numbered steps—clearly identified by a gray shaded background—students are constantly guided in solving the case problem. In addition, the numerous screen shots with callouts direct students' attention to what they should look at on the screen.

TROUBLE? Paragraphs These paragraphs anticipate the mistakes or problems that students may have and help them continue with the tutorial.

"Read This Before You Begin" Page Located opposite the first tutorial's opening page for each section of the text, the Read This Before You Begin Page helps introduce technology into the classroom. Technical considerations and assumptions about software are listed to save time and eliminate unnecessary aggravation. Notes about the Data Disks help instructors and students get their files in the right places, so students get started on the right foot.

Quick Check Questions Each session concludes with meaningful, conceptual Quick Check questions that test students' understanding of what they learned in the session. Answers to the Quick Check questions are provided at the end of each tutorial.

Reference Windows Reference Windows are succinct summaries of the most important tasks covered in a tutorial and they preview actions students will perform in the steps to follow.

Task Reference Located as a table at the end of the book, the Task Reference contains a summary of how to perform common tasks using the most efficient method, as well as references to pages where the task is discussed in more detail.

End-of-Tutorial Review Assignments, Case Problems, Internet Assignments, and Lab Assignments Review Assignments provide students with additional hands-on practice of the skills they learned in the tutorial using the same case presented in the tutorial. These assignments are followed by three to five Case Problems that have approximately the same scope as the tutorial case but use a different scenario. In addition, some of the Review Assignments or Case Problems may include Exploration Exercises that challenge students, encourage them to explore the capabilities of the program they are using, and/or further extend their knowledge. Each tutorial also includes instructions on getting to the text's Student Online Companion page, which contains the Internet Assignments and other related links for the text. Internet Assignments are additional exercises that integrate the skills the students learned in the tutorial with the World Wide Web. If a Course Lab accompanies a tutorial, Lab Assignments are included after the Case Problems.

New Perspectives on Microsoft® Access® 2000 — Brief Instructor's Resource Kit for this title contains:

- Electronic Instructor's Manual
- Data Files
- Solution Files
- Course Test Manager Testbank
- Course Test Manager Engine
- Figure Files

These supplements come on CD-ROM. If you don't have access to a CD-ROM drive, contact your Course Technology customer service representative for more information.

Acknowledgments

I would like to thank the dedicated and enthusiastic Course Technology staff, especially Rachel Crapser for her leadership; Jessica Evans for her excellence and positive attitude and influence and for going the extra mile; and Kathy Finnegan for her many contributions under very difficult circumstances. I wish the very best to Kathy, Connor and Devon.

Joseph J. Adamski

I would like to thank the following reviewers for their helpful feedback: Calleen Coorough, Skagit Valley College; Bonnie Bailey, Moorhead State; Rick Wilkerson, Dyersburg State Community College; Rebekah Tidwell, Carson-Newman College; and Carol Beck, College of St. Mary. My thanks to all the Course Technology staff, especially Rachel Crapser for her guidance and encouragement; Melissa Dezotell and Karen Shortill for their support; Daphne Barbas for her excellent management of the production process; and John Bosco, Quality Assurance Project leader, and Nicole Ashton, John Freitas, Alex White, and Jeff Schwartz, QA testers, for ensuring the accuracy of the text. Special thanks to Jessica Evans for her outstanding editorial and technical contributions in developing this text, and to Joe Adamski for lending his insights and expertise. This book is dedicated in loving memory to Joe and Jeff, who left us too soon; with all my love and gratitude to my parents, Ed and Mary, and my mother-in-law, Elaine; and with hope and love to my two beautiful sons, Connor and Devon.

Kathleen T. Finnegan

TABLE OF CONTENTS

Reference **Window List**

Tutorial Tips

These tutorials will help you learn about Microsoft Access 2000. The tutorials are designed to be worked through at a computer. Each tutorial is divided into sessions. Watch for the session headings, such as Session 1.1 and Session 1.2. Each session is designed to be completed in about 45 minutes, but take as much time as you need. It's also a good idea to take a break between sessions.

Before you begin, read the following questions and answers. They will help you plan your time and use the tutorials effectively.

Where do I start?

Each tutorial begins with a case, which sets the scene for the tutorial and gives you background information to help you understand what you will be doing. Read the case before you go to the lab. In the lab, begin with the first session of a tutorial.

How do I know what to do on the computer?

Each session contains steps that you will perform on the computer to learn how to use Microsoft Access 2000. Read the text that introduces each series of steps. The steps you need to do at a computer are numbered and are set against a shaded background. Read each step carefully and completely before you try it.

How do I know if I did the step correctly?

As you work, compare your computer screen with the corresponding figure in the tutorial. Don't worry if your screen display is somewhat different from the figure. The important parts of the screen display are labeled in each figure. Check to make sure these parts are on your screen.

What if I make a mistake?

Don't worry about making mistakes—they are part of the learning process. Paragraphs labeled "TROUBLE?" identify common problems and explain how to get back on track. Follow the steps in a TROUBLE? paragraph only if you are having the problem described. If you run into other problems:

- Carefully consider the current state of your system, the position of the pointer, and any messages on the screen.

- Complete the sentence, "Now I want to…" Be specific, because identifying your goal will help you rethink the steps you need to take to reach that goal.

- If you are working on a particular piece of software, consult the Help system.

- If the preceding suggestions don't solve your problem, consult your technical support person for assistance.

How do I use the Reference Windows?

Reference Windows summarize the procedures you will learn in the tutorial steps. Do not complete the actions in the Reference Windows when you are working through the tutorial. Instead, refer to the Reference Windows while you are working on the assignments at the end of the tutorial.

How can I test my understanding of the material I learned in the tutorial?

At the end of each session, you can answer the Quick Check questions. The answers for the Quick Checks are at the end of that tutorial.

After you have completed the entire tutorial, you should complete the Review Assignments and Case Problems. They are carefully structured so that you will review what you have learned and then apply your knowledge to new situations.

What if I can't remember how to do something?

You should refer to the Task Reference at the end of the book; it summarizes how to accomplish tasks using the most efficient method.

Before you begin the tutorials, you should know the basics about your computer's operating system. You should also know how to use the menus, dialog boxes, Help system, and My Computer.

Now that you've read the Tutorial Tips, you are ready to begin.

LEVEL I

New Perspectives on

MICROSOFT®
ACCESS® 2000

Read This Before You Begin

To the Student

Data Disks

To complete the Level I tutorials, Review Assignments, and Case Problems, you need 6 Data Disks. Your instructor will either provide you with these Data Disks or ask you to make your own.

If you are making your own Data Disks, you will need 6 blank, formatted high-density disks. You will need to copy a set of folders from a file server or standalone computer or the Web onto your disks. Your instructor will tell you which computer, drive letter, and folders contain the files you need. You could also download the files by going to www.course.com, clicking Data Disk Files, and following the instructions on the screen.

The following list shows you which folders go on each of your disks, so that you will have enough disk space to complete all the tutorials, Review Assignments, and Case Problems:

Data Disk 1
Write this on the disk label:
Data Disk 1: Tutorial files

Put this folder from the Disk 1 folder on the disk:
Tutorial

Data Disk 2
Write this on the disk label:
Data Disk 2: Review Assignments files

Put this folder from the Disk 2 folder on the disk:
Review

Data Disk 3
Write this on the disk label:
Data Disk 3: Case Problem 1 files

Put this folder from the Disk 3 folder on the disk:
Cases

Data Disk 4
Write this on the disk label:
Data Disk 4: Case Problem 2

Put this folder from the Disk 4 folder on the disk:
Cases

Data Disk 5
Write this on the disk label:
Data Disk 5: Case Problem 3

Put this folder from the Disk 5 folder on the disk:
Cases

Data Disk 6
Write this on the disk label:
Data Disk 6: Case Problem 4

Put this folder from the Disk 6 folder on the disk:
Cases

When you begin each tutorial, be sure you are using the correct Data Disk. Refer to the "File Finder" Chart at the back of this text for more detailed information on which files are used in which tutorials. These Access Level I tutorials use the same files for Tutorials 1-4. If you are completing the Level II tutorials, you will need to create new Data Disks for those tutorials. See the inside front or inside back cover of this book for more information on Data Disk files, or ask your instructor or technical support person for assistance.

Course Labs

The Access Level I tutorials feature an interactive Course Lab to help you understand database concepts. There are Lab Assignments at the end of Tutorial 1 that relate to this Lab.

To start a Lab, click the **Start** button on the Windows taskbar, point to **Programs**, point to **Course Labs**, point to **New Perspectives Course Labs**, and click the name of the Lab you want to use.

Using Your Own Computer

If you are going to work through this book using your own computer, you need:

- **Computer System** Microsoft Windows 95, 98, NT, or higher must be installed on your computer. This book assumes a typical installation of Microsoft Access.

- **Data Disks** You will not be able to complete the tutorials or exercises in this book using your own computer until you have your Data Disks.

- **Course Labs** See your instructor or technical support person to obtain the Course Lab software for use on your own computer.

Visit Our World Wide Web Site

Additional materials designed especially for you are available on the World Wide Web.
Go to http://www.course.com.

To the Instructor

The Data Files and Course Labs are available on the Instructor's Resource Kit for this title. Follow the instructions in the Help file on the CD-ROM to install the programs to your network or standalone computer. For information on creating Data Disks or the Course Labs, see the "To the Student" section above.

You are granted a license to copy the Data Files and Course Labs to any computer or computer network used by students who have purchased this book.

Databases and Relationships

A collection of related tables is called a **database**, or a **relational database**. Valle Coffee's Restaurant database will contain two related tables: the Customer table, which Barbara has already created, and the Order table, which you will create in Tutorial 2. Sometimes you might want information about customers and the orders they placed. To obtain this information you must have a way to connect records in the Customer table to records in the Order table. You connect the records in the separate tables through a **common field** that appears in both tables. In the sample database shown in Figure 1-2, each record in the Customer table has a field named Customer #, which is also a field in the Order table. For example, Oaks Restaurant is the fourth customer in the Customer table and has a Customer # of 635. This same Customer # field value, 635, appears in three records in the Order table. Therefore, Oaks Restaurant is the customer that placed these three orders.

Figure 1-2	DATABASE RELATIONSHIP BETWEEN TABLES FOR CUSTOMERS AND ORDERS

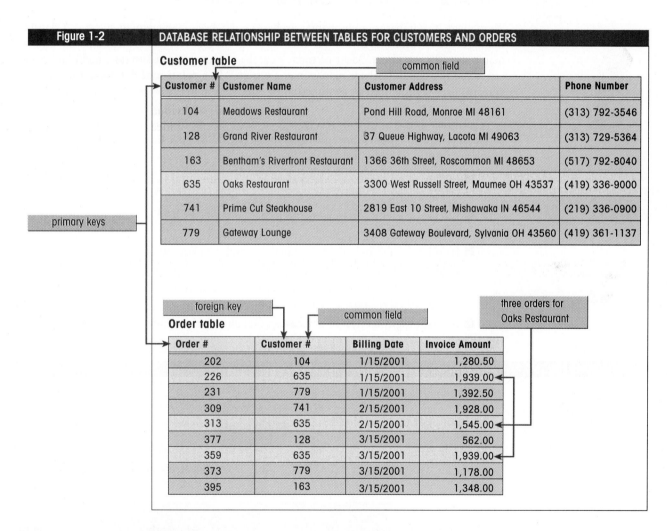

Customer table

common field

Customer #	Customer Name	Customer Address	Phone Number
104	Meadows Restaurant	Pond Hill Road, Monroe MI 48161	(313) 792-3546
128	Grand River Restaurant	37 Queue Highway, Lacota MI 49063	(313) 729-5364
163	Bentham's Riverfront Restaurant	1366 36th Street, Roscommon MI 48653	(517) 792-8040
635	Oaks Restaurant	3300 West Russell Street, Maumee OH 43537	(419) 336-9000
741	Prime Cut Steakhouse	2819 East 10 Street, Mishawaka IN 46544	(219) 336-0900
779	Gateway Lounge	3408 Gateway Boulevard, Sylvania OH 43560	(419) 361-1137

primary keys

foreign key

common field

three orders for Oaks Restaurant

Order table

Order #	Customer #	Billing Date	Invoice Amount
202	104	1/15/2001	1,280.50
226	635	1/15/2001	1,939.00
231	779	1/15/2001	1,392.50
309	741	2/15/2001	1,928.00
313	635	2/15/2001	1,545.00
377	128	3/15/2001	562.00
359	635	3/15/2001	1,939.00
373	779	3/15/2001	1,178.00
395	163	3/15/2001	1,348.00

Each Customer # in the Customer table must be unique, so that you can distinguish one customer from another and identify the customer's specific orders in the Order table. The Customer # field is referred to as the primary key of the Customer table. A **primary key** is a field, or a collection of fields, whose values uniquely identify each record in a table. In the Order table, Order # is the primary key.

When you include the primary key from one table as a field in a second table to form a relationship between the two tables, it is called a **foreign key** in the second table, as shown in Figure 1-2. For example, Customer # is the primary key in the Customer table and a foreign key in the Order table. Although the primary key Customer # has unique values in the Customer table, the same field as a foreign key in the Order table does not have unique values. The Customer # value 635, for example, appears three times in the Order table because the Oaks Restaurant placed three orders. Each foreign key value, however, must match one of the field values for the primary key in the other table. In the example shown in Figure 1-2, each Customer # value in the Order table must match a Customer # value in the Customer table. The two tables are related, enabling users to tie together the facts about customers with the facts about orders.

Relational Database Management Systems

To manage its databases, a company purchases a database management system. A **database management system (DBMS)** is a software program that lets you create databases and then manipulate data in them. Most of today's database management systems, including Access, are called relational database management systems. In a **relational database management system**, data is organized as a collection of tables. As stated earlier, a relationship between two tables in a relational DBMS is formed through a common field.

A relational DBMS controls the storage of databases on disk by carrying out data creation and manipulation requests. Specifically, a relational DBMS provides the following functions, which are illustrated in Figure 1-3:

- ■ It allows you to create database structures containing fields, tables, and table relationships.
- ■ It lets you easily add new records, change field values in existing records, and delete records.
- ■ It contains a built-in query language, which lets you obtain immediate answers to the questions you ask about your data.
- ■ It contains a built-in report generator, which lets you produce professional-looking, formatted reports from your data.
- ■ It provides protection of databases through security, control, and recovery facilities.

| Figure 1-3 | A RELATIONAL DATABASE MANAGEMENT SYSTEM |

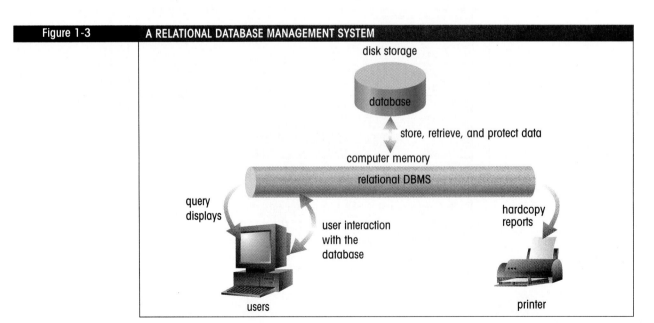

A company like Valle Coffee benefits from a relational DBMS because it allows several users working in different departments to share the same data. More than one user can enter data into a database, and more than one user can retrieve and analyze data that was entered by others. For example, Valle Coffee will keep only one copy of the Customer table, and all employees will be able to use it to meet their specific needs for customer information.

Finally, unlike other software programs, such as spreadsheets, a DBMS can handle massive amounts of data and can easily form relationships among multiple tables. Each Access database, for example, can be up to two gigabytes in size and can contain up to 32,768 objects (tables, queries, and so on).

Now that you've learned some database terms and concepts, you're ready to start Access and open the Restaurant database.

Starting Access

You start Access in the same way that you start other Windows programs—using the Start button on the taskbar.

To start Access:

1. Make sure Windows is running on your computer and the Windows desktop appears on your screen.

2. Click the **Start** button on the taskbar to display the Start menu, and then point to **Programs** to display the Programs menu.

3. Point to **Microsoft Access** on the Programs menu. See Figure 1-4.

Figure 1-4	STARTING MICROSOFT ACCESS

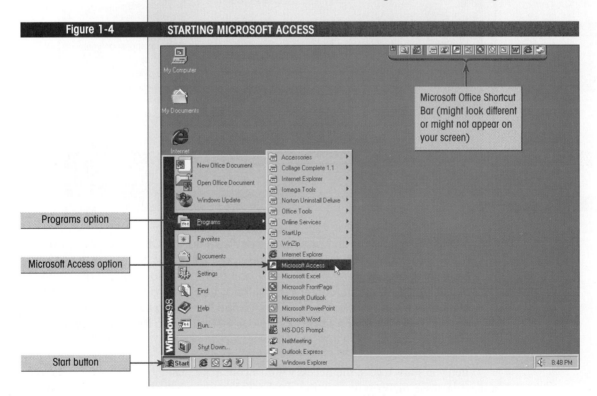

TROUBLE? Don't worry if your screen differs slightly from the figure. Although the figures in this book were created on a computer running Windows 98 in its default settings, the different Windows operating systems share the same basic user interface, and Microsoft Access runs equally well using Windows 95, Windows 98 in Web Style, Windows NT, or Windows 2000.

TROUBLE? If you don't see the Microsoft Access option on the Programs menu, ask your instructor or technical support person for help.

TROUBLE? The Office Shortcut Bar, which appears along the top border of the desktop in Figure 1-4, might look different on your screen, or it might not appear at all, depending on how your system is set up. Because these tutorials do not require you to use the Office Shortcut Bar, it has been omitted from the remaining figures in this text.

4. Click **Microsoft Access** to start Access. After a short pause, the Access copyright information appears in a message box and remains on the screen until the Access window is displayed. See Figure 1-5.

Figure 1-5	THE MICROSOFT ACCESS WINDOW

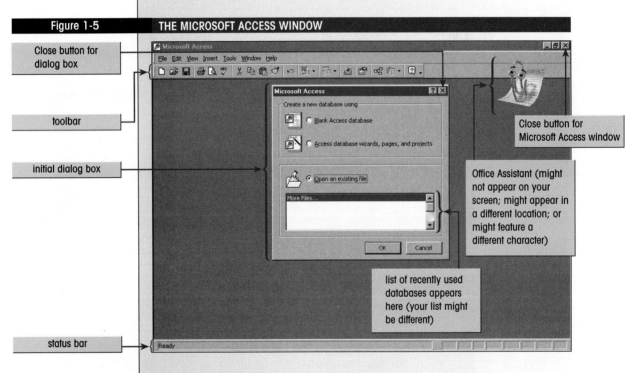

TROUBLE? Depending on how your system is set up, the Office Assistant (see Figure 1-5) might open when you start Access. If it opens, right-click the Office Assistant to display the shortcut menu, and then click Hide. You'll learn more about the Office Assistant later in this tutorial. If you've started Access immediately after installing it, you'll need to click the Start Using Microsoft Access option, which the Office Assistant displays, before hiding the Office Assistant.

When you start Access, the Access window contains a dialog box that allows you to create a new database or open an existing database. You can click the "Blank Access database" option button to create a new database on your own, or you can click the "Access database wizards, pages, and projects" option button and let a Wizard guide you through the steps for creating a database. In this case, you need to open an existing database.

Opening an Existing Database

To open an existing database, you can select the name of a database in the list of recently opened databases (if the list appears), or you can click the More Files option to open a database not listed. You need to open an existing database—the Restaurant database on your Data Disk.

To open the Restaurant database:

1. Make sure you have created your copy of the Access Data Disk, and then place your Data Disk in the appropriate disk drive.

TROUBLE? If you don't have a Data Disk, you need to get one before you can proceed. Your instructor will either give you one or ask you to make your own. (See your instructor for information.) In either case, be sure that you have made a backup copy of your Data Disk before you begin working, so that the original Data Files will be available on the copied disk in case you need to start over because of an error or problem.

2. In the Microsoft Access dialog box, make sure the **Open an existing file** option button is selected. Also, if your dialog box contains a list of files, make sure the **More Files** option is selected.

3. Click the **OK** button to display the Open dialog box. See Figure 1-6.

| Figure 1-6 | OPEN DIALOG BOX |

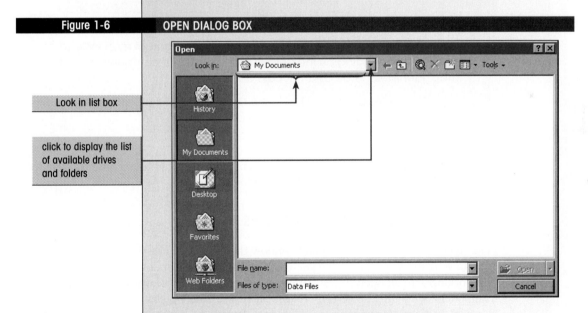

Look in list box

click to display the list of available drives and folders

TROUBLE? The list of folders and files on your screen might be different from the list in Figure 1-6, which does not contain any items.

4. Click the **Look in** list arrow, and then click the drive that contains your Data Disk.

5. Click **Tutorial** in the list box (if necessary), and then click the **Open** button to display a list of the files in the Tutorial folder.

6. Click **Restaurant** in the list box, and then click the **Open** button. The Restaurant database opens in the Access window. See Figure 1-7.

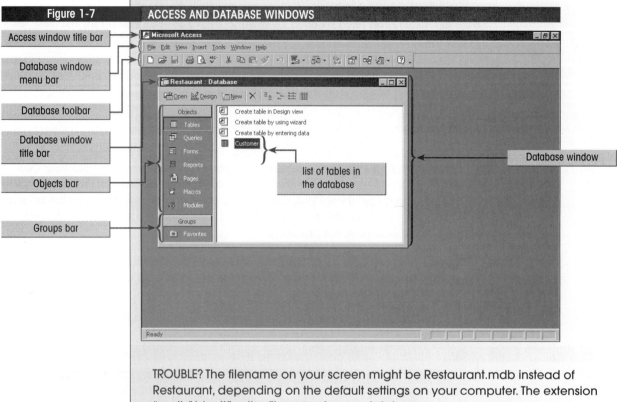

Figure 1-7   ACCESS AND DATABASE WINDOWS

TROUBLE? The filename on your screen might be Restaurant.mdb instead of Restaurant, depending on the default settings on your computer. The extension ".mdb" identifies the file as an Access database.

TROUBLE? If Tables is not selected in the Objects bar of the Database window, click it to display the list of tables in the database.

Before you can begin working with the database, you need to become familiar with the components of the Access and Database windows.

The Access and Database Windows

The **Access window** is the program window that appears when you start the program. The **Database window** appears when you open a database; this window is the main control center for working with an open Access database. Except for the Access window title bar, all screen components now on your screen are associated with the Database window (see Figure 1-7). Most of these screen components—including the title bars, window sizing buttons, menu bar, toolbar, and status bar—are the same as the components in other Windows programs.

The Database window provides a variety of options for viewing and manipulating database objects. Each item in the **Objects bar** controls one of the major object groups—such as tables, queries, forms, and reports—in an Access database. The **Groups bar** allows you to organize different types of database objects into groups, with shortcuts to those objects, so that you can work with them more easily.

The Database window also provides a toolbar with buttons for quickly creating, opening, and managing objects, as well as shortcut options for some of these tasks.

Barbara has already created the Customer table in the Restaurant database. She asks you to open the Customer table and view its contents.

Opening an Access Table

As noted earlier, tables contain all the data in a database. Tables are the fundamental objects for your work in Access. To view, add, change, or delete data in a table, you first must open the table. You can open any Access object by using the Open button in the Database window.

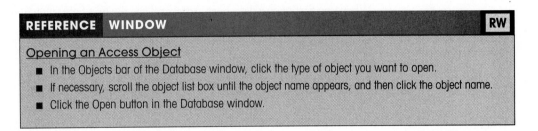

REFERENCE WINDOW **RW**

Opening an Access Object
- In the Objects bar of the Database window, click the type of object you want to open.
- If necessary, scroll the object list box until the object name appears, and then click the object name.
- Click the Open button in the Database window.

You need to open the Customer table, which is the only table currently in the Restaurant database.

To open the Customer table:

1. If the Customer table is not highlighted, click **Customer** to select it.

2. Click the **Open** button in the Database window. The Customer table opens in Datasheet view on top of the Database and Access windows. See Figure 1-8.

Figure 1-8   **TABLE DISPLAYED IN DATASHEET VIEW**

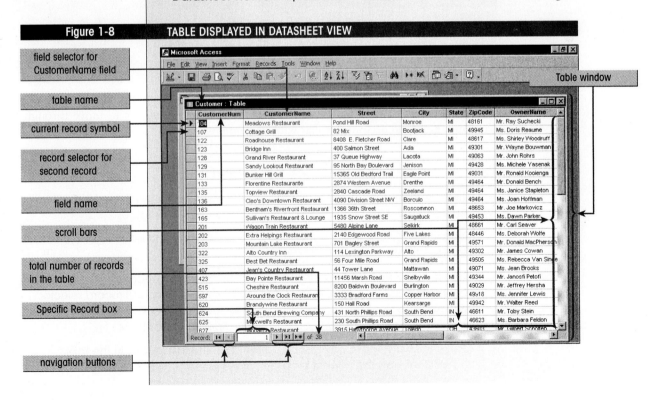

Datasheet view shows a table's contents as a **datasheet** in rows and columns, similar to a table or spreadsheet. Each row is a separate record in the table, and each column contains the field values for one field in the table. Each column is headed by a field name inside a field selector, and each row has a record selector to its left. Clicking a **field selector** or a **record selector** selects that entire column or row (respectively), which you can then manipulate. A field selector is also called a **column selector**, and a record selector is also called a **row selector**.

Navigating an Access Datasheet

When you first open a datasheet, Access selects the first field value in the first record. Notice that this field value is highlighted and that a darkened triangle symbol, called the current record symbol, appears in the record selector to the left of the first record. The **current record symbol** identifies the currently selected record. Clicking a record selector or field value in another row moves the current record symbol to that row. You can also move the pointer over the data on the screen and click one of the field values to position the insertion point.

The Customer table currently has nine fields and 38 records. To view fields or records not currently visible in the datasheet, you can use the horizontal and vertical scroll bars shown in Figure 1-8 to navigate through the data. The **navigation buttons**, also shown in Figure 1-8, provide another way to move vertically through the records. Figure 1-9 shows which record becomes the current record when you click each navigation button. The **Specific Record box**, which appears between the two sets of navigation buttons, displays the current record number. The total number of records in the table appears to the right of the navigation buttons.

Figure 1-9	NAVIGATION BUTTONS

NAVIGATION BUTTON	RECORD SELECTED	NAVIGATION BUTTON	RECORD SELECTED
◄◄	First Record	►►	Last Record
◄	Previous Record	►✳	New Record
►	Next Record		

Barbara suggests that you use the various navigation techniques to move through the Customer table and become familiar with its contents.

To navigate the Customer datasheet:

1. Click the right scroll arrow in the horizontal scroll bar a few times to scroll to the right and view the remaining fields in the Customer table.

2. Drag the scroll box in the horizontal scroll bar back to the left to return to the previous display of the datasheet.

3. Click the **Next Record** navigation button ►. The second record is now the current record, as indicated by the current record symbol in the second record selector. Also, notice that the second record's value for the CustomerNum field is highlighted, and "2" (for record number 2) appears in the Specific Record box.

4. Click the **Last Record** navigation button ►►. The last record in the table, record 38, is now the current record.

5. Click the **Previous Record** navigation button [◄]. Record 37 is now the current record.

6. Click the **First Record** navigation button [I◄]. The first record is now the current record.

Next, Barbara asks you to print the Customer table so that you can refer to it as you continue working with the Restaurant database.

Printing a Table

In Access you can print a table using either the Print command on the File menu or the Print button on the toolbar. The Print command opens a dialog box in which you can specify print settings. The Print button prints the table using the current settings. You'll use the Print button to print the Customer table.

To print the Customer table:

1. Click the **Print** button [🖫] on the Table Datasheet toolbar. Because all of the fields can't fit across one page, the table prints on two pages. You'll learn how to specify different print settings in later tutorials.

Now that you've viewed and printed the Customer table, you can exit Access.

Exiting Access

To exit Access, you simply click the Close button on the Access window title bar. When exiting, Access closes any open tables and the open database before closing the program.

To exit Access:

1. Click the **Close** button [✕] on the Access window title bar. The Customer table and the Restaurant database close, Access closes, and you return to the Windows desktop.

Now that you've become familiar with Access and the Restaurant database, you're ready to work with the data stored in the database.

Session 1.1 QUICK CHECK

1. A(n) _____ is a single characteristic of a person, place, object, event, or idea.

2. You connect the records in two separate tables through a(n) _____ that appears in both tables.

3. The _____, whose values uniquely identify each record in a table, is called a _____ when it is placed in a second table to form a relationship between the two tables.

4. In a table, the rows are called _____, and the columns are called _____.

5. The _____ identifies the selected record in an Access table.

6. Describe the two methods for navigating through a table.

SESSION 1.2

In this session, you will create and print a query; create and print a form; use the Help system; and create, preview, and print a report.

Kim Carpenter, the director of marketing at Valle Coffee, wants a list of all restaurant customers so that her staff can call customers to check on their satisfaction with Valle Coffee's services and products. She doesn't want the list to include all the fields in the Customer table (such as Street and ZipCode). To produce this list for Kim, you need to create a query using the Customer table.

Creating and Printing a Query

A **query** is a question you ask about the data stored in a database. In response to a query, Access displays the specific records and fields that answer your question. When you create a query, you tell Access which fields you need and what criteria Access should use to select the records. Then Access displays only the information you want, so you don't have to navigate through the entire database for the information.

You can design your own queries or use an Access **Query Wizard**, which guides you through the steps to create a query. The Simple Query Wizard allows you to select records and fields quickly, and is an appropriate choice for producing the customer list Kim wants.

To start the Simple Query Wizard:

1. Insert your Data Disk in the appropriate disk drive.

2. Start Access, make sure the **Open an existing file** option button is selected and the **More Files** option is selected, and then click the **OK** button to display the Open dialog box.

3. Click the **Look in** list arrow, click the drive that contains your Data Disk, click **Tutorial** in the list box, and then click the **Open** button to display the list of files in the Tutorial folder.

4. Click **Restaurant** in the list box, and then click the **Open** button.

5. Click **Queries** in the Objects bar of the Database window to display the Queries list. The Queries list box does not contain any queries yet.

You need to use the Simple Query Wizard to create the query for Kim. You can choose this Wizard either by clicking the New button, which opens a dialog box from which you can choose among several different Wizards to create your query, or by double-clicking the "Create query by using wizard" option, which automatically starts the Simple Query Wizard.

6. Double-click **Create query by using wizard**. The first Simple Query Wizard dialog box opens. See Figure 1-10.

Figure 1-10	FIRST SIMPLE QUERY WIZARD DIALOG BOX

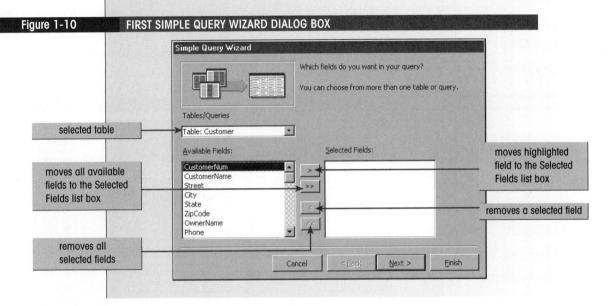

Because Customer is the only object currently in the Restaurant database, it is listed in the Tables/Queries box. You could click the Tables/Queries list arrow to choose another table or a query on which to base the query you're creating. The Available Fields list box lists the fields in the selected table (in this case, Customer). You need to select fields from this list to include them in the query. To select fields one at a time, click a field and then click the [>] button. The selected field moves from the Available Fields list box on the left to the Selected Fields list box on the right. To select all the fields, click the [>>] button. If you change your mind or make a mistake, you can remove a field by clicking it in the Selected Fields list box and then clicking the [<] button. To remove all selected fields, click the [<<] button.

Each Wizard dialog box contains buttons on the bottom that allow you to move to the previous dialog box (Back button), move to the next dialog box (Next button), or cancel the creation process (Cancel button) and return to the Database window. You can also finish creating the object (Finish button) and accept the Wizard's defaults for the remaining options.

Kim wants her list to include data from only the following fields: CustomerNum, CustomerName, City, State, OwnerName, and Phone. You need to select these fields to be included in the query.

To create the query using the Simple Query Wizard:

1. Click **CustomerNum** in the Available Fields list box (if necessary), and then click the [>] button. The CustomerNum field moves to the Selected Fields list box.

2. Repeat Step 1 for the fields **CustomerName**, **City**, **State**, **OwnerName**, and **Phone**, and then click the **Next** button. The second, and final, Simple Query Wizard dialog box opens and asks you to choose a name for your query. This name will appear in the Queries list in the Database window. You'll change the suggested name (Customer Query) to "Customer List."

3. Click at the end of the highlighted name, use the Backspace key to delete the word "Query," and then type **List**. Now you can view the query results.

4. Click the **Finish** button to complete the query. Access displays the query results in Datasheet view.

5. Click the **Maximize** button ▢ on the Query window to maximize the window. See Figure 1-11.

| Figure 1-11 | QUERY RESULTS |

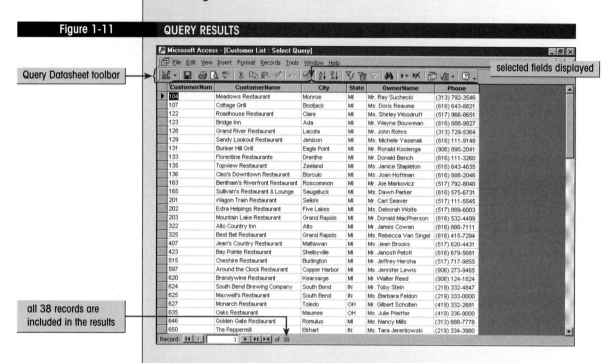

Query Datasheet toolbar

selected fields displayed

all 38 records are included in the results

The datasheet displays the six selected fields for each record in the Customer table. The fields are shown in the order you selected them, from left to right.

The records are currently listed in order by the primary key field (CustomerNum). Kim prefers the records to be listed in order by state so that her staff members can focus on all records for the customers in a particular state. To display the records in the order Kim wants, you need to sort the query results by the State field.

To sort the query results:

1. Click to position the insertion point anywhere in the State column. This establishes the State column as the current field.

2. Click the **Sort Ascending** button 🔡 on the Query Datasheet toolbar. Now the records are sorted in ascending alphabetical order by the values in the State field. All the records for Indiana are listed first, followed by the records for Michigan and then Ohio.

Kim asks for a printed copy of the query results so that she can bring the customer list to a meeting with her staff members. To print the query results, you can use the Print button on the Query Datasheet toolbar.

To print the query results:

1. Click the **Print** button 🖨 on the Query Datasheet toolbar to print one copy of the query results with the current settings.

2. Click the **Close** button ⊠ on the menu bar to close the query.

A dialog box opens and asks if you want to save changes to the design of the query. This box opens because you changed the sort order of the query results.

3. Click the **Yes** button to save the query design changes and return to the Database window. Notice that the Customer List query now appears in the Queries list box. In addition, because you maximized the Query window, now the Database window is also maximized. You need to restore the window.

4. Click the **Restore** button 🗗 on the menu bar to restore the Database window.

The query results are not stored in the database; however, the query design is stored as part of the database with the name you specified. You can re-create the query results at any time by running the query again. You'll learn more about creating and running queries in Tutorial 3.

After Kim leaves for her staff meeting, Barbara asks you to create a form for the Customer table so that her staff members can use the form to enter and work with data easily in the table.

Creating and Printing a Form

A **form** is an object you use to maintain, view, and print records in a database. Although you can perform these same functions with tables and queries, forms can present data in customized and useful ways.

In Access, you can design your own forms or use a Form Wizard to create forms for you automatically. A **Form Wizard** is an Access tool that asks you a series of questions, and then creates a form based on your answers. The quickest way to create a form is to use an **AutoForm Wizard**, which places all the fields from a selected table (or query) on a form automatically, without asking you any questions, and then displays the form on the screen.

Barbara wants a form for the Customer table that will show all the fields for one record at a time, with fields listed one below another. This type of form will make it easier for her staff to focus on all the data for a particular customer. You'll use the AutoForm: Columnar Wizard to create the form.

To create the form using an AutoForm Wizard:

1. Click **Forms** in the Objects bar of the Database window to display the Forms list. The Forms list box does not contain any forms yet.

2. Click the **New** button in the Database window to open the New Form dialog box. See Figure 1-12.

Figure 1-12	NEW FORM DIALOG BOX

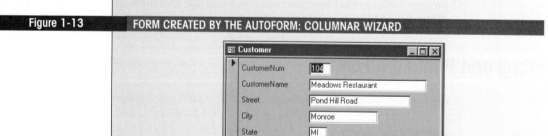

click to design your own form

Form Wizards

click to select the table or query for the form

The top list box provides options for designing your own form or creating a form using one of the Form Wizards. In the bottom list box, you choose the table or query that will supply the data for the form.

3. Click **AutoForm: Columnar** to select this AutoForm Wizard.

4. Click the list arrow for choosing the table or query on which to base the form, and then click **Customer**.

5. Click the **OK** button. The AutoForm Wizard creates the form and displays it in Form view. See Figure 1-13.

Figure 1-13	FORM CREATED BY THE AUTOFORM: COLUMNAR WIZARD

TROUBLE? The background of your form might look different from the one shown in Figure 1-13, depending on your computer's settings. If so, don't worry. You will learn how to change the form's style later in this text. For now, continue with the tutorial.

The form displays one record at a time in the Customer table. Access displays the field values for the first record in the table and selects the first field value (CustomerNum).

Each field name appears on a separate line and on the same line as its field value, which appears in a box. The widths of the boxes are different to accommodate the different sizes of the displayed field values; for example, compare the small box for the State field value with the larger box for the CustomerName field value. The AutoForm: Columnar Wizard automatically placed the field names and values on the form and supplied the background style.

Also, notice that the Form window contains navigation buttons, similar to those available in Datasheet view, which you can use to display different records in the form.

Barbara asks you to print the data for the Embers Restaurant, which is the last record in the table. After printing this record in the form, you'll save the form with the name "Customer Data" in the Restaurant database. Then the form will be available for later use. You'll learn more about creating and customizing forms in Tutorial 4.

To print the form with data for the last record, and then save and close the form:

1. Click the **Last Record** navigation button. The last record in the table, record 38 for Embers Restaurant, is now the current record.

2. Click **File** on the menu bar, and then click **Print**. The Print dialog box opens.

3. Click the **Selected Record(s)** option button, and then click the **OK** button to print only the current record in the form.

4. Click the **Save** button on the Form View toolbar. The Save As dialog box opens.

5. In the Form Name text box, click at the end of the highlighted word "Customer," press the **spacebar**, type **Data**, and then press the **Enter** key. Access saves the form as Customer Data in your Restaurant database and closes the dialog box.

6. Click the **Close** button on the Form window title bar to close the form and return to the Database window. Note that the Customer Data form is now listed in the Forms list box.

Kim returns from her staff meeting with another request. She wants the same customer list you produced earlier when you created the Customer List query, but she'd like the information presented in a more readable format. She suggests you use the Access Help system to learn about formatting data in reports.

Getting Help

The Access Help system provides the same options as the Help system in other Windows programs—the Help Contents, the Answer Wizard, and the Help Index—which are available from the Microsoft Access Help window. The Access Help system also provides additional ways to get help as you work—the Office Assistant and the What's This? command. You'll learn how to use the Office Assistant next in this section. The What's This? command provides context-sensitive Help information. When you choose this command from the Help menu, the pointer changes to the Help pointer, which you can then use to click any object or option on the screen to see a description of the object or option.

Finding Information with the Office Assistant

The Office Assistant is an interactive guide to finding information in the Help system. You can ask the Office Assistant a question, and then it will search the Help system to find an answer.

REFERENCE	WINDOW		RW

Using the Office Assistant

- Click the Microsoft Access Help button on any toolbar (or click Help on any menu bar, and then click Microsoft Access Help or Show the Office Assistant).
- Type your question in the text box provided by the Office Assistant, and then click the Search button.
- Choose a topic from the list of topics displayed by the Office Assistant. Click additional topics, as necessary.
- When finished, close the Help window and the Office Assistant.

You'll use the Office Assistant to get Help about creating reports in Access. Because you chose to hide the Office Assistant earlier in this tutorial, you need to redisplay it first.

To get Help about reports:

1. Click the **Microsoft Access Help** button ⌷ on the Database toolbar. The Office Assistant appears and displays a text box in which you can type your question. See Figure 1-14.

Figure 1-14	USING THE OFFICE ASSISTANT

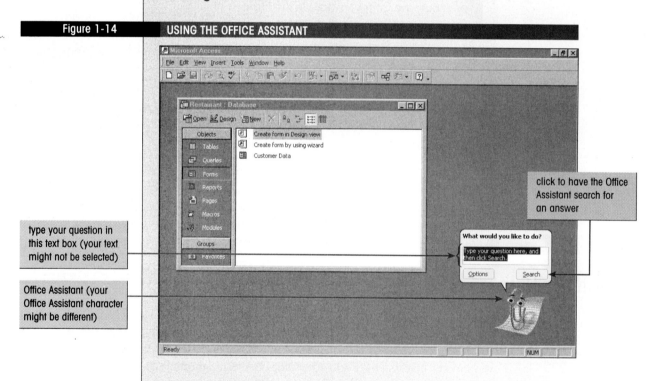

type your question in this text box (your text might not be selected)

Office Assistant (your Office Assistant character might be different)

click to have the Office Assistant search for an answer

TROUBLE? If the Microsoft Access Help window opens instead of the Office Assistant, click the Close button ⌷ to close the Help window, click Help on the menu bar, and then click Show the Office Assistant. If you don't see the text box and the Search button, click the Office Assistant.

TROUBLE? Your Office Assistant might appear in a different location on your screen. You can click and drag the Office Assistant to move it to another location, if you want.

You need to find information about creating reports in Access. To do so, you can simply begin to type your question.

2. Type **How do I create a report?** and then click the **Search** button. The Office Assistant displays a list of relevant topics. See Figure 1-15.

| Figure 1-15 | LIST OF RELATED TOPICS |

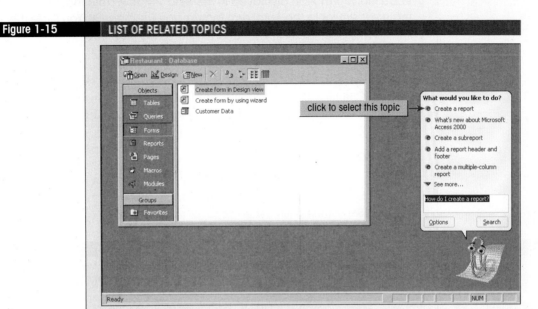

3. In the list of topics, click **Create a report**. The Office Assistant opens the topic in the Microsoft Access Help window, which opens on the left or right side of your screen. To see more of the Help window, you can maximize it.

4. Click the **Maximize** button 🗖 on the Microsoft Access Help window.

5. After reading the displayed text, click the topic **Create a report by using AutoReport** in the Help window. The Help window for using AutoReport opens. Because the Office Assistant might block the text in the Help window, you'll hide it again.

6. Right-click the **Office Assistant** to display the shortcut menu, click **Hide**, and then click anywhere in the Help window to redisplay the entire window, if necessary. The full text of the Help topic is now visible. See Figure 1-16.

| Figure 1-16 | HELP INFORMATION ON AUTOREPORT |

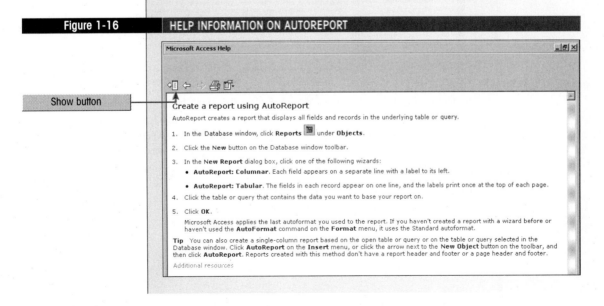

TROUBLE? If the Microsoft Access Help window minimizes when you hide the Office Assistant, click the Microsoft Access Help program button on the taskbar to restore the window.

7. Read the information displayed in the Help window. Note that the AutoReport feature is similar to the AutoForm feature you used earlier. You'll use the AutoReport: Columnar Wizard to create the report for Kim.

As mentioned earlier, the Help system in Access provides different ways to find information, including the Contents, Answer Wizard, and Index features. To gain access to these features, you need to use the Show button in the Microsoft Access Help window (see Figure 1-16).

To display the additional Help features:

1. Click the **Show** button 🔲 on the toolbar in the Microsoft Access Help window. The Contents, Answer Wizard, and Index tabs appear in the left frame of the window. See Figure 1-17.

Figure 1-17	ADDITIONAL HELP FEATURES

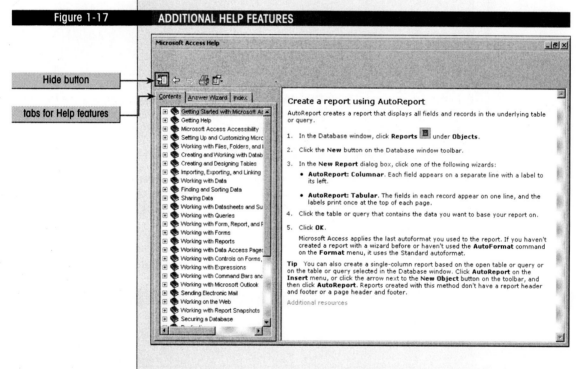

Note that the Show button is now labeled the Hide button, which you could click to remove the display of the tabs. You'll have a chance to use some of these additional Help tools in the exercises at the end of this tutorial. For now, you can close the Microsoft Access Help window and create the report for Kim.

2. Click the **Close** button ⊠ on the Microsoft Access Help window title bar to exit Help and return to the Database window.

Creating, Previewing, and Printing a Report

A **report** is a formatted printout (or screen display) of the contents of one or more tables in a database. Although you can print data from tables, queries, and forms, reports provide you with the greatest flexibility for formatting printed output.

Kim wants a report showing the same information contained in the Customer List query that you created earlier. However, she wants the data for each customer to be grouped together, with one customer record below another, as shown in the report sketch in Figure 1-18. You'll use the AutoReport: Columnar Wizard to produce the report for Kim.

Figure 1-18	SKETCH OF KIM'S REPORT

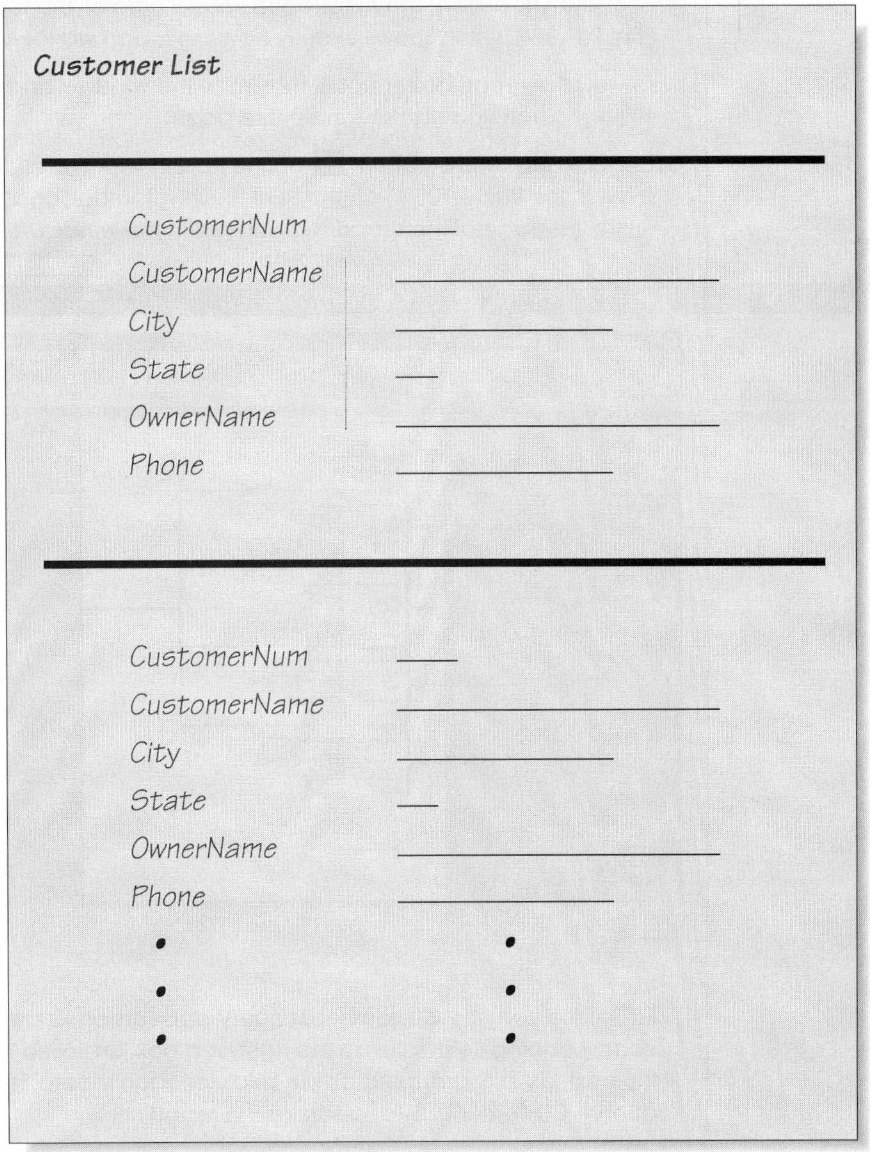

Customer List

CustomerNum   ——
CustomerName   _____
City   _____
State   ——
OwnerName   _____
Phone   _____

CustomerNum   ——
CustomerName   _____
City   _____
State   ——
OwnerName   _____
Phone   _____
           •   •
           •   •
           •   •

To create the report using the AutoReport: Columnar Wizard:

1. Click **Reports** in the Objects bar of the Database window, and then click the **New** button in the Database window to open the New Report dialog box, which is similar to the New Form dialog box you saw earlier.

2. Click **AutoReport: Columnar** to select this Wizard for creating the report.

   Because Kim wants the same data as in the Customer List query, you need to choose that query as the basis for the report.

3. Click the list arrow for choosing the table or query on which to base the report, and then click **Customer List**.

4. Click the **OK** button. The AutoReport Wizard creates the report and displays it in Print Preview, which shows exactly how the report will look when printed.

   To view the report better, you'll maximize the window and change the Zoom setting so that you can see the entire page.

5. Click the **Maximize** button 🔲 on the Report window, click the **Zoom** list arrow (next to the value 100%) on the Print Preview toolbar, and then click **Fit**. The entire first page of the report is displayed in the window. See Figure 1-19.

Figure 1-19	FIRST PAGE OF THE REPORT IN PRINT PREVIEW

report title taken from query name

fields grouped for each record

lines separate records

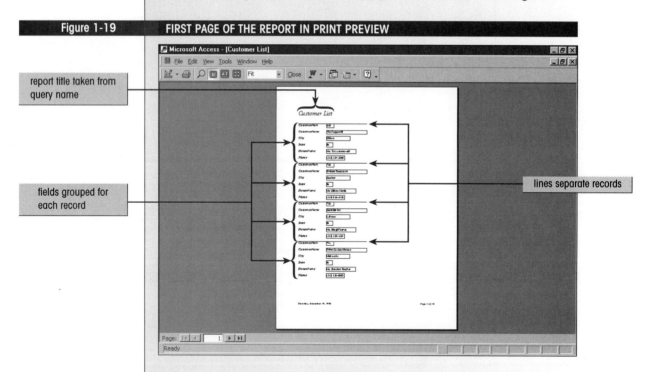

Each field from the Customer List query appears on its own line, with the corresponding field value to the right, in a box. Lines separate one record from the next, visually grouping all the fields for each record. The name of the query—Customer List—appears as the report title.

TROUBLE? The background of your report might look different from the one shown in Figure 1-19, depending on your computer's settings. If so, don't worry. You will learn how to change the report's style later in this text.

The report spans multiple pages. Kim asks you to print just the first page of the report so that she can review its format. After printing the report page, you'll close the report without saving it because you can easily re-create it at any time. In general, it's best to save an object—report, form, or query—only if you anticipate using the object frequently or if it is time-consuming to create, because these objects use considerable storage space on your disk. You'll learn more about creating and customizing reports in Tutorial 4.

To print the first report page, and then close the report:

1. Click **File** on the menu bar, and then click **Print**. The Print dialog box opens. You need to change the print settings to print only the first page of the report.

2. In the Print Range section, click the **Pages** option button, type **1** in the From text box, press the **Tab** key, and then type **1** in the To text box.

3. Click the **OK** button to print the first page of the report. Now you can close the report.

4. Click the **Close** button ☒ on the menu bar. *Do not* click the Close button on the Print Preview toolbar.

   TROUBLE? If you clicked the Close button on the Print Preview toolbar, you switched to Design view. Simply click the Close button ☒ on the menu bar, and then continue with the tutorial.

   A dialog box opens and asks if you want to save the changes to the report design.

5. Click the **No** button to close the report without saving it.

When you work in an Access database and create and manipulate objects, such as queries, forms, and reports, the size of your database increases. To free up disk space and make a database a more manageable size, Access provides a way for you to compact a database.

Compacting a Database

Whenever you open an Access database and work in it, the size of the database increases. Likewise, when you delete records or database objects—such as queries, forms, and reports—the space occupied by the deleted records or objects on disk does not become available for other records or objects. To make the space available, you must compact the database. **Compacting** a database rearranges the data and objects in a database to make its size smaller. Unlike making a copy of a database file, which you do to protect your database against loss or damage, you compact a database to make it smaller, thereby making more space available on your disk.

Compacting and Repairing a Database

When you compact a database, Access repairs the database at the same time. In many cases, Access detects that a database is damaged when you try to open it and gives you the option to compact and repair it at that time. If you think your database might be damaged because it is behaving unpredictably, you can use the "Compact and Repair Database" option to fix it. With your database file open, choose the Database Utilities option from the Tools menu, and then choose the Compact and Repair Database option.

Compacting a Database Automatically

Access also allows you to set an option for your database file so that every time you close the database, it will be compacted automatically.

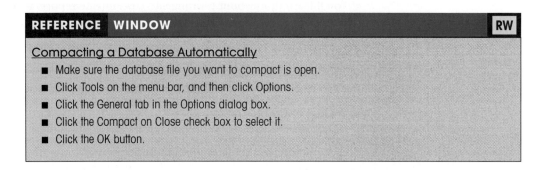

REFERENCE WINDOW   **RW**

Compacting a Database Automatically
- Make sure the database file you want to compact is open.
- Click Tools on the menu bar, and then click Options.
- Click the General tab in the Options dialog box.
- Click the Compact on Close check box to select it.
- Click the OK button.

You'll set the compact option now for the Restaurant database. Then, every time you subsequently open and close the Restaurant database, Access will compact the database file for you. After setting this option, you'll exit Access.

To set the option for compacting the Restaurant database:

1. Make sure the Restaurant Database window is open on your screen.

2. Click **Tools** on the menu bar, and then click **Options**. The Options dialog box opens.

3. Click the **General** tab in the dialog box, and then click the **Compact on Close** check box to select it. See Figure 1-20.

Figure 1-20   **GENERAL TAB OF THE OPTIONS DIALOG BOX**

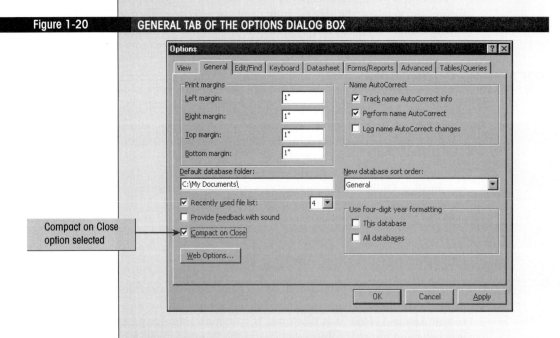

4. Click the **OK** button to set the option. Now you can exit Access.

5. Click the **Close** button ⊠ on the Access window title bar to exit Access. When you exit, Access closes the Restaurant database file and compacts it automatically.

Backing Up and Restoring a Database

As noted earlier, you make a backup copy of a database file to protect your database against loss or damage. You can make the backup copy using one of several methods: Windows Explorer, My Computer, Microsoft Backup, or other backup software. If you back up your database file to a floppy disk, and the file size exceeds the size of the disk, you cannot use Windows Explorer or My Computer; you must use Microsoft Backup or some other backup software so that you can copy the file over more than one disk.

To restore a database file that you have backed up, choose the same method you used to make the backup copy. For example, if you used the Microsoft Backup tool (which is one of the System Tool Accessories available from the Programs menu), you must choose the Restore option for this tool to copy the database file to your database folder. If the existing database file and the backup copy have the same name, restoring the backup copy might replace the existing file. If you want to save the existing file, rename it before you restore it.

With the Customer table in place, Barbara can continue to build the Restaurant database and use it to store, manipulate, and retrieve important data for Valle Coffee. In the following tutorials, you'll help Barbara complete and maintain the database, and you'll use it to meet the specific information needs of other Valle Coffee employees.

Session 1.2 QUICK CHECK

1. A(n) _____ is a question you ask about the data stored in a database.

2. Unless you specify otherwise, the records resulting from a query are listed in order by the _____.

3. The quickest way to create a form is to use a(n) _____.

4. Describe the form created by the AutoForm: Columnar Wizard.

5. Describe how you use the Office Assistant to get Help.

6. After creating a report, the AutoReport Wizard displays the report in _____.

REVIEW ASSIGNMENTS

In the Review Assignments, you'll work with the **Customer** database, which is similar to the database you worked with in the tutorial. Complete the following:

1. Make sure your Data Disk is in the disk drive.

2. Start Access and open the **Customer** database, which is located in the Review folder on your Data Disk.

Explore 3. In the Microsoft Access Help window, display and then click the Contents tab. (*Hint*: Click any topic displayed in the Office Assistant list box to open the Microsoft Access Help window.) Double-click the topic "Creating and working with Databases." Click the topic "Databases: What they are and how they work," and then click the related graphic for the topic. Read the displayed information. When finished, close the window to return to the Contents tab. Repeat this procedure for the similarly worded topics for tables, queries, forms, and reports. When finished reading all the topics, close the Microsoft Access Help window.

Explore

4. Use the Office Assistant to ask the following question: "How do I rename a table?" Choose the topic "Rename a database object" and read the displayed information. Close the Microsoft Access Help window and hide the Office Assistant. Then, in the **Customer** database, rename the **Table1** table as **Customers**.

5. Open the **Customers** table.

Explore

6. In the Microsoft Access Help window, display and then click the Index tab. (*Hint*: Click any topic displayed in the Office Assistant list box to open the Help window.) Type the keyword "print" in the Type keywords text box, and then click the Search button. Click the topic "Print a report." Read the displayed information, click the button for more information at the end of the first paragraph (>>), and then read the information. Close the Microsoft Access Help window. Print the **Customers** table datasheet in landscape orientation. Close the **Customers** table.

7. Use the Simple Query Wizard to create a query that includes the City, CustomerName, OwnerName, and Phone fields (in that order) from the **Customers** table. Name the query **Customer Phone List**. Sort the query results in ascending order by City. Print the query results, and then close and save the query.

8. Use the AutoForm: Columnar Wizard to create a form for the **Customers** table.

Explore

9. Use context-sensitive Help to find out how to move to a particular record and display it in the form. Click the What's This? command from the Help menu, and then use the Help pointer to click the number 1 in the Specific Record box at the bottom of the form. Read the displayed information. Click to close the Help box, and then use the Specific Record box to move to record 28 (for The Peppermill) in the **Customers** table.

10. Print the form for the current record (28), save the form as **Customer Info**, and then close the form.

Explore

11. Use the AutoReport: Tabular Wizard to create a report based on the **Customers** table. Print the first page of the report, and then close and save the report as **Customers**.

12. Set the option for compacting the **Customer** database on close.

13. Exit Access.

CASE PROBLEMS

Case 1. Ashbrook Mall Information Desk   Ashbrook Mall is a large, modern mall located in Phoenix, Arizona. The Mall Operations Office is responsible for everything that happens within the mall and anything that affects the mall's operation. Among the independent operations groups that report to the Mall Operations Office are the Maintenance Group, the Mall Security Office, and the Information Desk. You will be helping the Information Desk personnel.

One important service provided by the Information Desk is to maintain a catalog of current job openings at stores within the mall. Sam Bullard, the director of the Mall Operations Office, recently created an Access database named **MallJobs** to store this information. You'll help Sam complete and maintain this database. Complete the following:

1. Make sure your Data Disk is in the disk drive.

2. Start Access and open the **MallJobs** database, which is located in the Cases folder on your Data Disk.

3. Open the **Store** table, print the table datasheet, and then close the table.

4. Use the Simple Query Wizard to create a query that includes the StoreName, Contact, and Extension fields (in that order) from the **Store** table. Name the query **Contact List**. Print the query results, and then close the query.

Explore   5. Use the AutoForm: Tabular Wizard to create a form for the **Store** table. Print the form, save it as **Store Info**, and then close it.

Explore   6. Use the AutoReport: Columnar Wizard to create a report based on the **Store** table. Maximize the Report window and change the Zoom setting to Fit. Use the Two Pages button on the Print Preview toolbar to view both pages of the report in Print Preview. Print the first page of the report, and then close and save it as **Stores**.

7. Set the option for compacting the **MallJobs** database on close.

8. Exit Access.

Case 2. *Professional Litigation User Services*   Professional Litigation User Services (PLUS) is a company that creates all types of visual aids for judicial proceedings. Clients are usually private law firms, although the District Attorney's office has occasionally contracted for its services. PLUS creates graphs, maps, timetables, and charts, both for computerized presentations and in large-size form for presentation to juries. PLUS also creates videos, animations, presentation packages, and slide shows—in short, anything of a visual nature that can be used in a judicial proceeding to make, clarify, or support a point.

Raj Jawahir, a new employee at PLUS, is responsible for tracking the daily payments received from the firm's clients. He created an Access database named **Payments**, and needs your help in working with this database. Complete the following:

1. Make sure your Data Disk is in the disk drive.

2. Start Access and open the **Payments** database, which is located in the Cases folder on your Data Disk.

3. Open the **Firm** table, print the table datasheet, and then close the table.

4. Use the Simple Query Wizard to create a query that includes the FirmName, PLUSAcctRep, and Extension fields (in that order) from the **Firm** table. Name the query **AcctRep List**.

Explore   5. Sort the query results in descending order by the PLUSAcctRep field. (*Hint*: Use a toolbar button.)

Explore   6. Use the Office Assistant to ask the following question: "How do I select multiple records?" Click the topic "Selecting fields and records in Datasheet view." Hide the Office Assistant, read the displayed information, and then close the Help window. Select the first 10 records in the datasheet (all the records with the value "Tyler, Olivia" in the PLUSAcctRep field), and then print just the selected records. Close the query, and save your changes to the design.

7. Use the AutoForm: Columnar Wizard to create a form for the **Firm** table. Move to record 25, and then print the form for the current record only. Save the form as **Firm Info** and then close the form.

8. Use the AutoReport: Columnar Wizard to create a report based on the **Firm** table. Maximize the Report window and change the Zoom setting to Fit.

Explore   9. Use the View menu to view all eight pages of the report at the same time in Print Preview.

10. Print just the first page of the report, and then close and save the report as **Firms**.

11. Set the option for compacting the **Payments** database on close.

12. Exit Access.

Case 3. Best Friends   Best Friends is a not-for-profit organization that trains hearing and service dogs for people with disabilities. Established in 1989 in Boise, Idaho, by Noah and Sheila Warnick, Best Friends is modeled after Paws With A Cause®, the original and largest provider of hearing and service dogs in the United States. Like Paws With A Cause® and other such organizations, Best Friends strives to provide "Dignity Through Independence."

To raise funds for Best Friends, Noah and Sheila periodically conduct walk-a-thons. The events have become so popular that Noah and Sheila created an Access database named **Walks** to track walker and pledge data. You'll help them complete and maintain the **Walks** database. Complete the following:

1. Make sure your Data Disk is in the disk drive.

2. Start Access and open the **Walks** database, which is located in the Cases folder on your Data Disk.

3. Open the **Walker** table, print the table datasheet, and then close the table.

Explore   4. Use the Simple Query Wizard to create a query that includes all the fields in the **Walker** table *except* the Phone field. (*Hint*: Use the `>>` and `<` buttons to select the necessary fields.) In the second Simple Query Wizard dialog box, make sure the Detail option button is selected. (This second dialog box opens because the table contains numeric values.) Name the query **Walker Distance**.

Explore   5. Sort the results in descending order by the Distance field. (*Hint*: Use a toolbar button.) Print the query results, and then close and save the query.

6. Use the AutoForm: Columnar Wizard to create a form for the **Walker** table. Move to record 16, and then print the form for the current record only. Save the form as **Walker Info**, and then close it.

7. Use the AutoReport: Columnar Wizard to create a report based on the **Walker** table. Maximize the Report window and change the Zoom setting to Fit.

Explore   8. Use the View menu to view all six pages of the report at the same time in Print Preview.

9. Print just the first page of the report, and then close and save the report as **Walkers**.

10. Set the option for compacting the **Walks** database on close.

11. Exit Access.

Case 4. Lopez Lexus Dealerships   Maria and Hector Lopez own a chain of Lexus dealerships throughout Texas. They have used a computer in their business for several years to handle payroll and typical accounting functions. Because of the dealership's phenomenal expansion, both in the number of car locations and the number of cars handled, they created an Access database named **Lexus** to track their car inventory. You'll help them work with and maintain this database. Complete the following:

1. Make sure your Data Disk is in the disk drive.

2. Start Access and open the **Lexus** database, which is located in the Cases folder on your Data Disk.

3. Open the **Cars** table.

Explore   4. Print the **Cars** table datasheet in landscape orientation, and then close the table.

Explore

5. Use the Simple Query Wizard to create a query that includes the Model, Class, Year, LocationCode, Cost, and SellingPrice fields (in that order) from the **Cars** table. In the second Simple Query Wizard dialog box, make sure the Detail option button is selected. (This second dialog box opens because the table contains numeric values.) Name the query **Cost vs Selling**.

Explore

6. Sort the query results in descending order by SellingPrice. (*Hint*: Use a toolbar button.)

7. Print the query results, and then close and save the query.

8. Use the AutoForm: Columnar Wizard to create a form for the **Cars** table. Move to record 3, and then print the form for the current record only. Save the form as **Car Info**, and then close it.

Explore

9. Use the AutoReport: Tabular Wizard to create a report based on the **Cars** table. Maximize the Report window and change the Zoom setting to Fit. Use the Two Pages button on the Print Preview toolbar to view both pages of the report in Print Preview. Print the first page of the report in landscape orientation, and then close and save the report as **Cars**.

10. Set the option for compacting the **Lexus** database on close.

11. Exit Access.

INTERNET ASSIGNMENTS

The purpose of the Internet Assignments is to challenge you to find information on the Internet that you can use to create effective documents. The actual assignments are updated and maintained on the Course Technology Web site. Log on to the Internet and use your Web browser to go to the Student Online Companion to accompany this text at **www.course.com/NewPerspectives/office2000**. Click the Access link, and then click the link for Tutorial 1.

LAB ASSIGNMENTS

Databases

These Lab Assignments are designed to accompany the interactive Course Lab called Databases. To start the Databases Lab, click the Start button on the Windows taskbar, point to Programs, point to Course Labs, point to New Perspectives Applications, and then click Databases. If you do not see Course Labs on your Programs menu, see your instructor or technical support person.

Databases   This Databases Lab demonstrates the essential concepts of file and database management systems. You will use the Lab to search, sort, and report the data contained in a file of classic books.

1. Click the Steps button to review basic database terminology and to learn how to manipulate the classic books database. As you proceed through the Steps, answer all of the Quick Check questions that appear. After you complete the Steps, you will see a Quick Check summary report. Follow the instructions on the screen to print this report.

2. Click the Explore button. Make sure you can apply basic database terminology to describe the classic books database by answering the following questions:

   a. How many records does the file contain?
   b. How many fields does each record contain?
   c. What are the contents of the Catalog # field for the book written by Margaret Mitchell?
   d. What are the contents of the Title field for the record with Thoreau in the Author field?
   e. Which field has been used to sort the records?

3. In Explore, manipulate the database as necessary to answer the following questions:

   a. When the books are sorted by title, what is the first record in the file?
   b. Use the Search button to search for all the books in the West location. How many do you find?
   c. Use the Search button to search for all the books in the Main location that are checked in. What do you find?

4. Use the Report button to print out a report that groups the books by Status and sorts them by Title. On your report, circle the four field names. Draw a box around the summary statistics showing which books are currently checked in and which books are currently checked out.

QUICK | CHECK ANSWERS

Session 1.1

1. field

2. common field

3. primary key; foreign key

4. records; fields

5. current record symbol

6. Use the horizontal and vertical scroll bars to view fields or records not currently visible in the datasheet; use the navigation buttons to move vertically through the records.

Session 1.2

1. query

2. primary key

3. AutoForm Wizard

4. The form displays each field name on a separate line to the left of its field value, which appears in a box; the widths of the boxes represent the size of the fields.

5. Click the Microsoft Access Help button on any toolbar (or choose Microsoft Access Help or Show the Office Assistant from the Help menu), type a question in the text box, click the Search button, and then choose a topic from the list displayed.

6. Print Preview

OBJECTIVES

In this tutorial you will:

- Learn the guidelines for designing databases and Access tables

- Create and save a table

- Define fields and specify the primary key

- Add records to a table

- Modify the structure of a table

- Delete, move, and add fields

- Change field properties

- Copy records from another Access database

- Delete and change records

MAINTAINING A DATABASE

Creating, Modifying, and Updating an Order Table

CASE

Valle Coffee

The Restaurant database currently contains only one table—the Customer table—which stores data about Valle Coffee's restaurant customers. Barbara Hennessey also wants to track information about each order placed by each restaurant customer. This information includes the order's billing date and invoice amount. Barbara asks you to create a second table in the Restaurant database, named Order, in which to store the order data.

Some of the order data Barbara needs is already stored in another Valle Coffee database. After creating the Order table and adding some records to it, you'll copy the records from the other database into the Order table. Then you'll maintain the Order table by modifying it and updating it to meet Barbara's specific data requirements.

SESSION 2.1

In this session, you will learn the guidelines for designing databases and Access tables. You'll also learn how to create a table, define the fields for a table, select the primary key for a table, save the table structure, and add records to a table datasheet.

Guidelines for Designing Databases

A database management system can be a useful tool, but only if you first carefully design the database so that it meets the needs of its users. In database design, you determine the fields, tables, and relationships needed to satisfy the data and processing requirements. When you design a database, you should follow these guidelines:

■ **Identify all the fields needed to produce the required information**. For example, Barbara needs information about customers and orders. Figure 2-1 shows the fields that satisfy those information requirements.

Figure 2-1	BARBARA'S DATA REQUIREMENTS

CustomerName	BillingDate
OrderNum	OwnerName
Street	InvoiceAmt
City	PlacedBy
State	Phone
ZipCode	FirstContact
CustomerNum	

■ **Group related fields into tables.** For example, Barbara grouped the fields relating to customers into the Customer table. The other fields are grouped logically into the Order table, which you will create, as shown in Figure 2-2.

Figure 2-2	BARBARA'S FIELDS GROUPED INTO CUSTOMER AND ORDER TABLES

Customer table	Order table
CustomerNum	OrderNum
CustomerName	BillingDate
Street	PlacedBy
City	InvoiceAmt
State	
ZipCode	
OwnerName	
Phone	
FirstContact	

■ **Determine each table's primary key.** Recall that a primary key uniquely identifies each record in a table. Although a primary key is not mandatory in Access, it's usually a good idea to include one in each table. Without a primary key, selecting the exact record you want can be a problem. For some tables, one of the fields, such as a Social Security number or credit card number, naturally serves the function of a primary key. For other tables, two or more fields might be needed to function as the primary key.

In these cases, the primary key is referred to as a **composite key**. For example, a school grade table would use a combination of student number and course code to serve as the primary key. For a third category of tables, no single field or combination of fields can uniquely identify a record in a table. In these cases, you need to add a field whose sole purpose is to serve as the primary key.

For Barbara's tables, CustomerNum is the primary key for the Customer table, and OrderNum will be the primary key for the Order table.

- **Include a common field in related tables.** You use the common field to connect one table logically with another table. For example, Barbara's Customer and Order tables will include the CustomerNum field as a common field. Recall that when you include the primary key from one table as a field in a second table to form a relationship, the field is called a foreign key in the second table; therefore, the CustomerNum field will be a foreign key in the Order table. With this common field, Barbara can find all orders placed by a customer; she can use the CustomerNum value for a customer and search the Order table for all orders with that CustomerNum value. Likewise, she can determine which customer placed a particular order by searching the Customer table to find the one record with the same CustomerNum value as the corresponding value in the Order table.

- **Avoid data redundancy.** Data redundancy occurs when you store the same data in more than one place. With the exception of common fields to connect tables, you should avoid redundancy because it wastes storage space and can cause inconsistencies, if, for instance, you type a field value one way in one table and a different way in the same table or in a second table. Figure 2-3 shows an example of incorrect database design that illustrates data redundancy in the Order table; the Customer Name field is redundant, and one value was entered incorrectly, in three different ways.

Figure 2-3	INCORRECT DATABASE DESIGN WITH DATA REDUNDANCY

■ **Determine the properties of each field.** You need to identify the **properties**, or characteristics, of each field so that the DBMS knows how to store, display, and process the field. These properties include the field's name, maximum number of characters or digits, description, valid values, and other field characteristics. You will learn more about field properties later in this tutorial.

The Order table you need to create will contain the fields shown in Figure 2-2. Before you create the table, you first need to learn some guidelines for designing Access tables.

Guidelines for Designing Access Tables

As just noted, the last step of database design is to determine the properties, such as the name and data type, of each field. Access has rules for naming fields, choosing data types, and defining other properties for fields.

Naming Fields and Objects

You must name each field, table, and other object in an Access database. Access then stores these items in the database, using the names you supply. It's best to choose a field or object name that describes the purpose or contents of the field or object, so that later you can easily remember what the name represents. For example, the two tables in the Restaurant database will be named Customer and Order, because these names suggest their contents.

The following rules apply to naming fields and objects:

■ A name can be up to 64 characters long.

■ A name can contain letters, numbers, spaces, and special characters, except for a period (.), exclamation mark (!), accent grave (`), and square brackets ([ ]).

■ A name cannot start with a space.

■ A table or query name must be unique within a database. A field name must be unique within a table, but it can be used again in another table.

In addition, experienced users of databases follow these tips for naming fields and objects:

■ Capitalize the first letter of each word in the name.

■ Avoid extremely long names because they are difficult to remember and reference.

■ Use standard abbreviations, such as Num for Number, Amt for Amount, and Qty for Quantity.

■ Do not use spaces in field names because these names will appear in column headings on datasheets and on labels on forms and reports. By not using spaces you'll be able to show more fields on these objects at one time.

Assigning Field Data Types

You must assign a data type for each field. The **data type** determines what field values you can enter for the field and what other properties the field will have. For example, the Order table will include a BillingDate field, so you will assign the date/time data type to this field because it will store date values. Then Access will allow you to enter and manipulate only dates or times as values in the BillingDate field.

Figure 2-4 lists the 10 data types available in Access, describes the field values allowed for each data type, explains when you should use each data type, and indicates the field size of each data type.

Figure 2-4	DATA TYPES FOR FIELDS	
DATA TYPE	**DESCRIPTION**	**FIELD SIZE**
Text	Allows field values containing letters, digits, spaces, and special characters. Use for names, addresses, descriptions, and fields containing digits that are not used in calculations.	0 to 255 characters; 50 characters default
Memo	Allows field values containing letters, digits, spaces, and special characters. Use for long comments and explanations.	1 to 64,000 characters; exact size is determined by entry
Number	Allows positive and negative numbers as field values. Numbers can contain digits, a decimal point, commas, a plus sign, and a minus sign. Use for fields that you will use in calculations, except calculations involving money.	1 to 15 digits
Date/Time	Allows field values containing valid dates and times from January 1, 100 to December 31, 9999. Dates can be entered in mm/dd/yy (month, day, year) format, several other date formats, or a variety of time formats such as 10:35 PM. You can perform calculations on dates and times, and you can sort them. For example, you can determine the number of days between two dates.	8 bytes
Currency	Allows field values similar to those for the number data type. Unlike calculations with number data type decimal values, calculations performed using the currency data type are not subject to round-off error.	Accurate to 15 digits on the left side of the decimal separator and to 4 digits on the right side
AutoNumber	Consists of integers with values controlled by Access. Access automatically inserts a value in the field as each new record is created. You can specify sequential numbering or random numbering. This guarantees a unique field value, so that such a field can serve as a table's primary key.	9 digits
Yes/No	Limits field values to yes and no, on and off, or true and false. Use for fields that indicate the presence or absence of a condition, such as whether an order has been filled, or if an employee is eligible for the company dental plan.	1 character
OLE Object	Allows field values that are created in other programs as objects, such as photographs, video images, graphics, drawings, sound recordings, voice-mail messages, spreadsheets, and word-processing documents. These objects can be linked or embedded.	1 gigabyte maximum; exact size depends on object size
Hyperlink	Consists of text used as a hyperlink address. A hyperlink address can have up to three parts: the text that appears in a field or control; the path to a file or page; and a location within the file or page. Hyperlinks help you to connect your application easily to the Internet or an intranet.	Up to 64,000 characters total for the three parts of a hyperlink data type
Lookup Wizard	Creates a field that lets you look up a value in another table or in a predefined list of values.	Same size as the primary key field used to perform the lookup

Assigning Field Sizes

The **field size** property defines a field value's maximum storage size for text, number, and AutoNumber fields only. The other data types have no field size property because their storage size is either a fixed, predetermined amount or is determined automatically by the field value itself, as shown in Figure 2-4. A text field has a default field size of 50 characters; you can also set its field size by entering a number in the range 1 to 255. For example, the OrderNum and CustomerNum fields in the Order table will be text fields with sizes of 3 each.

When you use the number data type to define a field, you should set the field's Field Size property based on the largest value that you expect to store in that field. Access processes smaller data sizes faster using less memory, so you can optimize your database's performance and its storage space by selecting the correct field size for each field. For example, it would be wasteful to use the Long Integer setting when defining a field that will only store whole numbers ranging from 0 to 255, because the Long Integer setting will use four bytes of storage space. A better choice would be the Byte setting, which uses one byte of storage space to store the same values. Other Field Size property settings for number fields are:

- **Byte**: Stores whole numbers (numbers with no fractions) from 0 to 255 in one byte
- **Integer**: Stores whole numbers from -32,768 to 32,767 in two bytes
- **Long Integer** (default): Stores whole numbers from -2,147,483,648 to 2,147,483,647 in four bytes
- **Single**: Stores positive and negative numbers to precisely seven decimal places and uses four bytes
- **Double**: Stores positive and negative numbers to precisely 15 decimal places and uses eight bytes
- **Replication ID**: Establishes a unique identifier for replication of tables, records, and other objects and uses 16 bytes
- **Decimal**: Stores positive and negative numbers to precisely 28 decimal places and uses 12 bytes

Barbara documented the design for the Order table by listing each field's name, data type, size (if applicable), and description, as shown in Figure 2-5. Note that Barbara assigned the text data type to the OrderNum field (the table's primary key), to the CustomerNum field (a foreign key to the Customer table), and to the PlacedBy field. BillingDate will have the date/time data type, and InvoiceAmt will have the currency data type.

Figure 2-5	DESIGN FOR THE ORDER TABLE			
Field Name	Data Type	Field Size	Description	
OrderNum	Text	3	primary key	
CustomerNum	Text	3	foreign key	
BillingDate	Date/Time			
PlacedBy	Text	25	person who placed order	
InvoiceAmt	Currency			

With Barbara's design, you are ready to create the Order table.

Creating a Table

Creating a table consists of naming the fields and defining the properties for the fields, specifying a primary key (and a foreign key, if applicable) for the table, and then saving the table structure. You will use Barbara's design (Figure 2-5) as a guide for creating the Order table. First, you need to open the Restaurant database.

To open the Restaurant database:

1. Place your Data Disk in the appropriate disk drive.

2. Start Access. The Access window opens with the initial dialog box.

3. Make sure that the **Open an existing file** option button and the **More Files** option are selected, and then click the **OK** button to display the Open dialog box.

4. Click the **Look in** list arrow, and then click the drive that contains your Data Disk.

5. Click **Tutorial** in the list box, and then click the **Open** button to display a list of the files in the Tutorial folder.

6. Click **Restaurant** in the list box, and then click the **Open** button. The Restaurant database opens in the Access window.

7. Make sure that **Tables** is selected in the Objects bar of the Database window.

The Customer table is listed in the Tables list box. Now you'll create the Order table in the Restaurant database.

To begin creating the Order table:

1. Click the **New** button in the Database window. The New Table dialog box opens. See Figure 2-6.

Figure 2-6	NEW TABLE DIALOG BOX

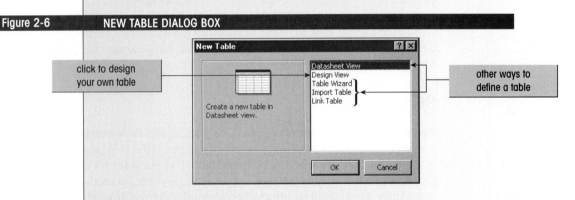

In Access, you can create a table from entered data (Datasheet View), define your own table (Design View), use a Wizard to automate the table creation process (Table Wizard), or use a Wizard to import or link data from another database or other data source (Import Table or Link Table). For the Order table, you will define your own table.

2. Click **Design View** in the list box, and then click the **OK** button. The Table window opens in Design view. See Figure 2-7.

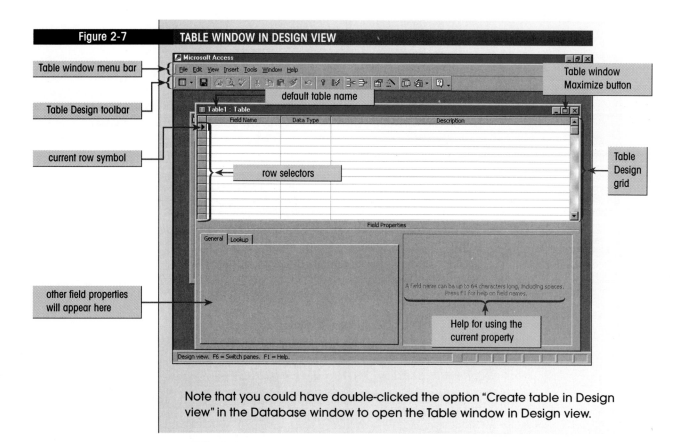

Figure 2-7   TABLE WINDOW IN DESIGN VIEW

Note that you could have double-clicked the option "Create table in Design view" in the Database window to open the Table window in Design view.

You use Design view to define or modify a table structure or the properties of the fields in a table. If you create a table without using a Wizard, you enter the fields and their properties for your table directly in this window.

Defining Fields

Initially, the default table name, Table1, appears on the Table window title bar, the current row symbol is positioned in the first row selector of the Table Design grid, and the insertion point is located in the first row's Field Name box. The purpose or characteristics of the current property (Field Name, in this case) appear in the lower-right section of the Table window. You can display more complete information about the current property by pressing the F1 key.

You enter values for the Field Name, Data Type, and Description field properties in the upper half of the Table window. You select values for all other field properties, most of which are optional, in the lower half of the window. These other properties will appear when you move to the first row's Data Type text box.

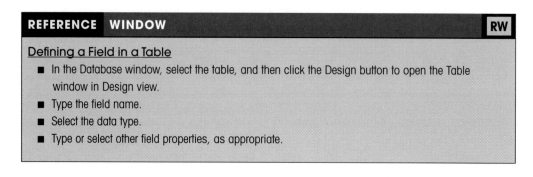

REFERENCE WINDOW   RW

Defining a Field in a Table
- In the Database window, select the table, and then click the Design button to open the Table window in Design view.
- Type the field name.
- Select the data type.
- Type or select other field properties, as appropriate.

The first field you need to define is OrderNum.

To define the OrderNum field:

1. Type **OrderNum** in the first row's Field Name text box, and then press the **Tab** key (or press the **Enter** key) to advance to the Data Type text box. The default data type, Text, appears highlighted in the Data Type text box, which now also contains a list arrow, and field properties for a text field appear in the lower half of the window. See Figure 2-8.

Figure 2-8	TABLE WINDOW AFTER ENTERING THE FIRST FIELD NAME

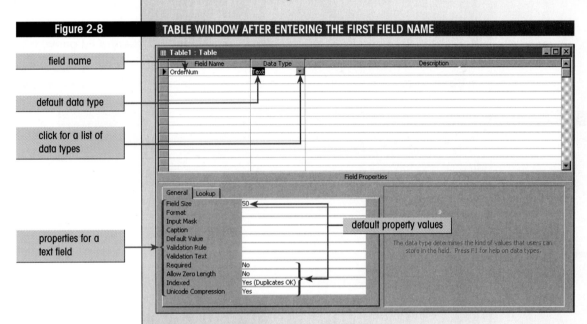

field name

default data type

click for a list of data types

properties for a text field

default property values

Notice that the lower-right section of the window now provides an explanation for the current property, Data Type.

TROUBLE? If you make a typing error, you can correct it by clicking the mouse to position the insertion point, and then using either the Backspace key to delete characters to the left of the insertion point or the Delete key to delete characters to the right of the insertion point. Then type the correct text.

Because order numbers will not be used for calculations, you will assign the text data type to the OrderNum field instead of the number data type, and then enter the Description property value as "primary key." You can use the Description property to enter an optional description for a field to explain its purpose or usage. A field's Description property can be up to 255 characters long, and its value appears in the status bar when you view the table datasheet.

2. Press the **Tab** key to accept Text as the field's data type and move to the Description text box, and then type **primary key** in the Description text box.

The Field Size property has a default value of 50, which you will change to a value of 3, because order numbers at Valle Coffee contain three digits. When you select or enter a value for a property, you *set* the property. The Required property has a default value of No, which means that a value does not need to be entered for the field. Because Barbara doesn't want an order entered without an order number, you will change the Required property to Yes. (Refer to the Access Help system for a complete description of all the properties available for the different data types.)

3. Select **50** in the Field Size text box either by dragging the pointer or double-clicking the mouse, and then type **3**.

4. Click the **Required** text box to position the insertion point there. A list arrow appears on the right side of the Required text box.

5. Click the **Required** list arrow. Access displays the Required list box. See Figure 2-9.

Figure 2-9	DEFINING THE ORDERNUM FIELD

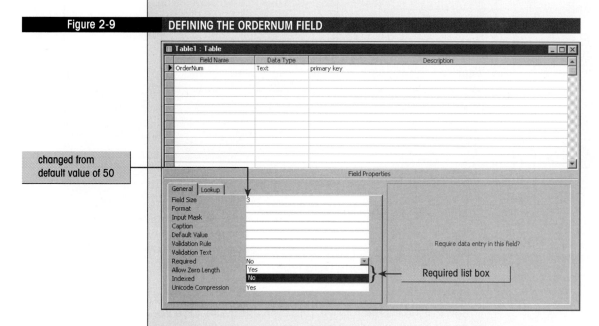

When you position the insertion point or select text in many Access text boxes, Access displays a list arrow, which you can click to display a list box with options. You can display the list arrow and the list box simultaneously if you click the text box near its right side.

6. Click **Yes** in the list box. The list box closes, and Yes is now the value for the Required property. The definition of the first field is complete.

Barbara's Order table design shows CustomerNum as the second field. You will define CustomerNum as a text field with a Description of "foreign key" and a Field Size of 3, because customer numbers at Valle Coffee contain three digits. Because it's possible that a record for an order might need to be entered for a customer not yet added to the database, Barbara asks you to leave the Required property at its default value of No.

To define the CustomerNum field:

1. Place the insertion point in the second row's Field Name text box, type **CustomerNum** in the text box, and then press the **Tab** key to advance to the Data Type text box.

   Customer numbers are not used in calculations, so you'll assign the text data type to the field, and then enter its Description value as "foreign key."

2. Press the **Tab** key to accept Text as the field's data type and to move to the Description text box, and then type **foreign key** in the Description text box.

   Next, you'll change the Field Size property to 3. Note that when defining the fields in a table, you can move between the top and bottom panes of the table window by pressing the F6 key.

3. Press the **F6** key to move to the bottom pane (Field Properties). The current entry for the Field Size property, 50, is highlighted.

4. Type **3** to set the Field Size property. You have completed the definition of the second field. See Figure 2-10.

Figure 2-10	TABLE WINDOW AFTER DEFINING THE FIRST TWO FIELDS

current field

property values set for the current field

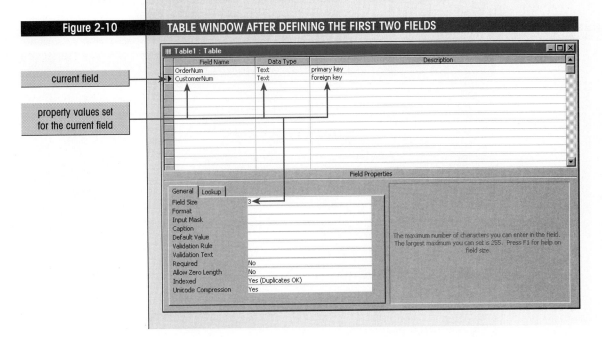

Using Barbara's Order table design in Figure 2-5, you can now complete the remaining field definitions: BillingDate with the date/time data type, PlacedBy with the text data type, and InvoiceAmt with the currency data type.

To define the BillingDate field:

1. Place the insertion point in the third row's Field Name text box, type **BillingDate** in the text box, and then press the **Tab** key to advance to the Data Type text box.

2. Click the **Data Type** list arrow, click **Date/Time** in the list box, and then press the **Tab** key to advance to the Description text box.

If you've assigned a descriptive field name and the field does not fulfill a special function (such as primary key), you usually do not enter a value for the optional Description property. BillingDate is a field that does not require a value for its Description property.

Barbara wants the values in the BillingDate field to be displayed in a format showing the month, day, and year as in the following example: 01/15/2001. You use the Format property to control the display of a field value.

3. In the Field Properties section, click the right side of the **Format** text box to display the list of predefined formats. As noted in the right section of the window, you can either choose a predefined format or enter a custom format.

TROUBLE? If you see a list arrow instead of a list of predefined formats, click the list arrow to display the list.

None of the predefined formats matches the layout Barbara wants for the BillingDate values. Therefore, you need to create a custom date format. Figure 2-11 shows some of the symbols available for custom date and time formats. (A complete description of all the custom formats is available in Help.)

Figure 2-11	SYMBOLS FOR SOME CUSTOM DATE FORMATS
SYMBOL	**DESCRIPTION**
/	date separator
d	day of the month in one or two numeric digits, as needed (1 to 31)
dd	day of the month in two numeric digits (01 to 31)
ddd	first three letters of the weekday (Sun to Sat)
dddd	full name of the weekday (Sunday to Saturday)
w	day of the week (1 to 7)
ww	week of the year (1 to 53)
m	month of the year in one or two numeric digits, as needed (1 to 12)
mm	month of the year in two numeric digits (01 to 12)
mmm	first three letters of the month (Jan to Dec)
mmmm	full name of the month (January to December)
yy	last two digits of the year (01 to 99)
yyyy	full year (0100 to 9999)

Barbara wants the dates to be displayed with a two-digit month (mm), a two-digit day (dd), and a four-digit year (yyyy). You'll enter this custom format now.

4. Click the **Format** list arrow to close the list of predefined formats, and then type **mm/dd/yyyy** in the Format text box. See Figure 2-12.

Figure 2-12	SPECIFYING THE CUSTOM DATE FORMAT

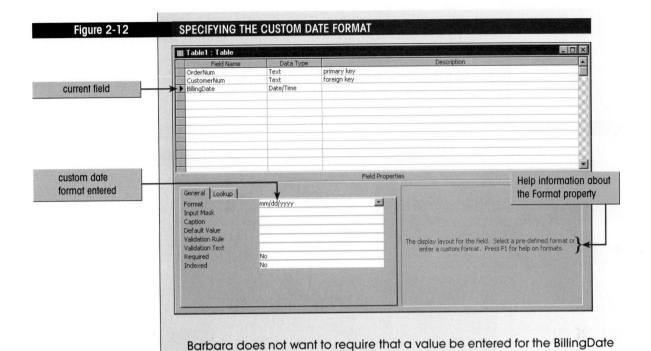

current field

custom date format entered

Help information about the Format property

Barbara does not want to require that a value be entered for the BillingDate field, so you have completed the definition of the field.

Now you're ready to finish the Order table design by defining the PlacedBy and InvoiceAmt fields.

To define the PlacedBy and InvoiceAmt fields:

1. Place the insertion point in the fourth row's Field Name text box.

2. Type **PlacedBy** in the Field Name text box, and then press the **Tab** key to advance to the Data Type text box.

   This field will contain names, so you'll assign the text data type to it. Also, Barbara wants to include the description "person who placed order" to clarify the contents of the field.

3. Press the **Tab** key to accept Text as the field's data type and to move to the Description text box, and then type **person who placed order** in the Description text box.

   Next, you'll change the Field Size property's default value of 50 to 25, which should be long enough to accommodate all names.

4. Press the **F6** key to move to and select 50 in the Field Size text box, and then type **25**.

   The definition of the PlacedBy field is complete. Next, you'll define the fifth and final field, InvoiceAmt. This field will contain dollar amounts, so you'll assign the currency data type to it.

5. Place the insertion point in the fifth row's Field Name text box.

6. Type **InvoiceAmt** in the Field Name text box, and then press the **Tab** key to advance to the Data Type text box.

You can select a value from the Data Type list box as you did for the BillingDate field. Alternatively, you can type the property value in the text box or type just the first character of the property value.

7. Type **c**. The value in the fifth row's Data Type text box changes to "currency," with the letters "urrency" highlighted. See Figure 2-13.

| Figure 2-13 | SELECTING A VALUE FOR THE DATA TYPE PROPERTY |

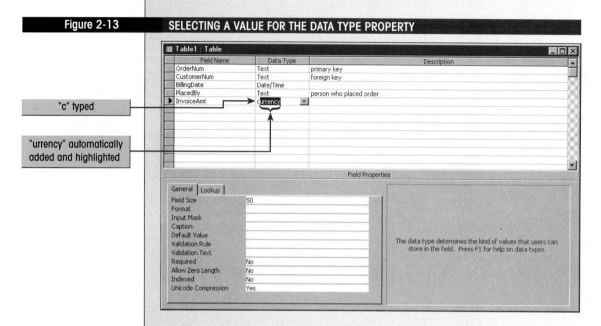

"c" typed

"urrency" automatically added and highlighted

8. Press the **Tab** key to advance to the Description text box. Access changes the value for the Data Type property to Currency.

In the Field Properties section, notice the default values for the Format, Decimal Places, and Default Value properties. For a field with a Format property value of Currency, two decimal places are provided when the Decimal Places property value is set to Auto. These properties, combined with the Default Value property of 0, specify that values in the InvoiceAmt field will initially appear as follows: $0.00. This is the format Barbara wants for the InvoiceAmt field, so you are finished defining the fields for the Order table.

Next, you need to specify the primary key for the Order table.

Specifying the Primary Key

Although Access does not require a table to have a primary key, including a primary key offers several advantages:

■ A primary key uniquely identifies each record in a table.

■ Access does not allow duplicate values in the primary key field. If a record already exists with an OrderNum value of 143, for example, Access prevents you from adding another record with this same value in the OrderNum field. Preventing duplicate values ensures the uniqueness of the primary key field.

■ Access forces you to enter a value for the primary key field in every record in the table. This is known as **entity integrity**. If you do not enter a value for a field, you have actually given the field what is known as a **null value**. You cannot give a null value to the primary key field because entity integrity prevents Access from accepting and processing that record.

■ Access stores records on disk in the same order as you enter them but displays them in order by the field values of the primary key. If you enter records in no specific order, you are ensured that you will later be able to work with them in a more meaningful, primary key sequence.

■ Access responds faster to your requests for specific records based on the primary key.

REFERENCE WINDOW   **RW**

Specifying a Primary Key for a Table
■ In the Table window in Design view, click the row selector for the field you've chosen to be the primary key.
■ If the primary key will consist of two or more fields, press and hold down the Ctrl key, and then click the row selector for each field.
■ Click the Primary Key button on the Table Design toolbar.

According to Barbara's design, you need to specify OrderNum as the primary key for the Order table.

To specify OrderNum as the primary key:

1. Position the pointer on the row selector for the OrderNum field until the pointer changes to ➡. See Figure 2-14.

| Figure 2-14 | SPECIFYING ORDERNUM AS THE PRIMARY KEY |

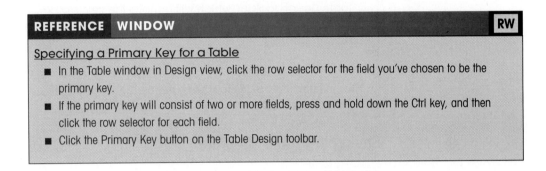

2. Click the mouse button. The entire first row of the Table Design grid is highlighted.

3. Click the **Primary Key** button 🔑 on the Table Design toolbar, and then click to the right of InvoiceAmt in the fifth row's Field Name text box to deselect the first row. A key symbol appears in the row selector for the first row, indicating that the OrderNum field is the table's primary key. See Figure 2-15.

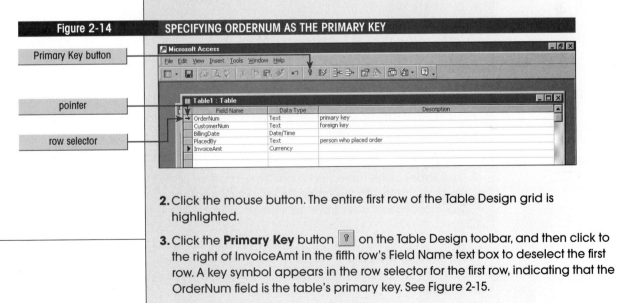

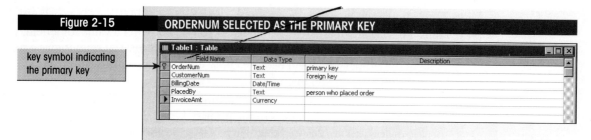

Figure 2-15

ORDERNUM SELECTED AS THE PRIMARY KEY

key symbol indicating
the primary key

Field Name	Data Type	Description
OrderNum	Text	primary key
CustomerNum	Text	foreign key
BillingDate	Date/Time	
PlacedBy	Text	person who placed order
InvoiceAmt	Currency	

If you specify the wrong field as the primary key, or if you later change your
mind and do not want the designated primary key field to be the primary key,
you simply need to select the field and then click the Primary Key button on the
Table Design toolbar, which will remove the key symbol and the primary key
designation from the field. Then you can choose another field to be the primary
key, if necessary.

You've defined the fields for the Order table and specified its primary key, so you can now
save the table structure.

Saving the Table Structure

The last step in creating a table is to name the table and save the table's structure on disk.
Once the table is saved, you can use it to enter data in the table.

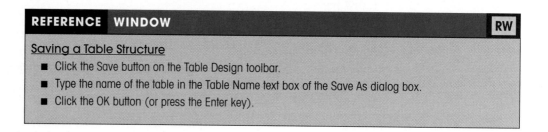

REFERENCE WINDOW   **RW**

Saving a Table Structure
- Click the Save button on the Table Design toolbar.
- Type the name of the table in the Table Name text box of the Save As dialog box.
- Click the OK button (or press the Enter key).

You need to save the table you've defined as "Order."

To name and save the Order table:

1. Click the **Save** button 📁 on the Table Design toolbar. The Save As dialog
   box opens.

2. Type **Order** in the Table Name text box, and then press the **Enter** key. Access
   saves the table with the name Order in the Restaurant database on your Data
   Disk. Notice that Order appears instead of Table1 in the Table window title bar.

Next, Barbara asks you to add the two records shown in Figure 2-16 to the Order
table. These two records contain data for orders that two customers recently placed with
Valle Coffee.

Figure 2-16	RECORDS TO BE ADDED TO THE ORDER TABLE				
	OrderNum	CustomerNum	BillingDate	PlacedBy	InvoiceAmt
	323	624	02/15/2001	Isabelle Rouy	$1,986.00
	201	107	01/15/2001	Matt Gellman	$854.00

Adding **Records to a Table**

You can add records to an Access table in several ways. A table datasheet provides a simple way for you to add records. As you learned in Tutorial 1, a datasheet shows a table's contents in rows and columns. Each row is a separate record in the table, and each column contains the field values for one field in the table. To view a table datasheet, you first must change from Design view to Datasheet view.

You'll switch to Datasheet view and add the two records in the Order table datasheet.

To add the records in the Order table datasheet:

1. Click the **View** button for Datasheet view 🔲 on the Table Design toolbar. The Table window opens in Datasheet view. See Figure 2-17.

Figure 2-17	TABLE WINDOW IN DATASHEET VIEW

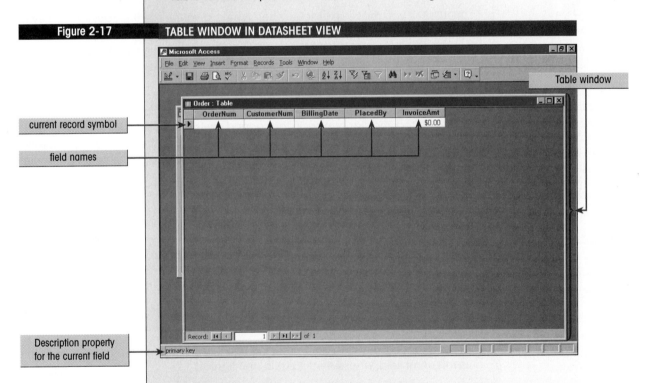

The table's five field names appear at the top of the datasheet. The current record symbol in the first row's record selector identifies the currently selected record, which contains no data until you enter the first record. The insertion point is located in the first row's OrderNum field, whose Description property appears in the status bar.

2. Type **323**, which is the first record's OrderNum field value, and then press the **Tab** key. Each time you press the Tab key, the insertion point moves to the right to the next field in the record. See Figure 2-18.

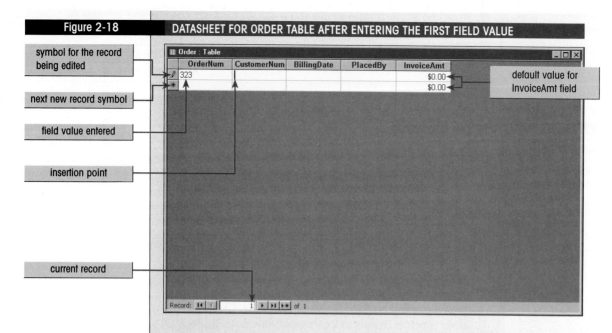

Figure 2-18   DATASHEET FOR ORDER TABLE AFTER ENTERING THE FIRST FIELD VALUE

- symbol for the record being edited
- next new record symbol
- field value entered
- insertion point
- current record
- default value for InvoiceAmt field

TROUBLE? If you make a mistake when typing a value, use the Backspace key to delete characters to the left of the insertion point, or the Delete key to delete characters to the right of the insertion point. Then type the correct text. If you want to correct a value by replacing it entirely, double-click the value to select it, and then type the correct value.

The pencil symbol in the first row's record selector indicates that the record is being edited. The star symbol in the second row's record selector identifies the second row as the next one available for a new record. The InvoiceAmt column displays "$0.00," the default value for the field, as specified by the field's properties.

3. Type **624** and then press the **Tab** key. The insertion point moves to the right side of the BillingDate field.

Recall that you specified a custom format for the BillingDate field, mm/dd/yyyy. However, when you enter the digits for the year, you only need to enter the final two digits; you do not have to enter all four digits. For example, for a field value containing the year 1999, you only need to enter "99" and Access will store and automatically display the full four digits, as specified by the custom format.

4. Type **02/15/01** and then press the **Tab** key. Access displays the BillingDate field value as "02/15/2001" and the insertion point moves to the PlacedBy field.

5. Type **Isabelle Rouy** and then press the **Tab** key. The insertion point moves to the InvoiceAmt field, whose field value is highlighted.

Notice that field values for text fields are left-aligned in their boxes, and field values for date/time and currency fields are right-aligned in their boxes. If the default value of $0.00 is correct for the InvoiceAmt field, you can press the Tab key to accept the value and advance to the beginning of the next record. Otherwise, type the field value for the InvoiceAmt field. You do not need to type the dollar sign, commas, or decimal point (for whole dollar amounts) because Access adds these symbols automatically for you.

6. Type **1986** and then press the **Tab** key. Access displays $1,986.00 for the InvoiceAmt field, stores the first completed record in the Order table, removes the pencil symbol from the first row's record selector, advances the insertion point to the second row's OrderNum text box, and places the current record symbol in the second row's record selector.

Now you can enter the values for the second record.

7. Type **201** in the OrderNum field, press the **Tab** key to move to the CustomerNum field, type **107** in the CustomerNum field, and then press the **Tab** key. The insertion point moves to the right side of the BillingDate field.

8. Type **01/15/01** and then press the **Tab** key. The insertion point moves to the PlacedBy field.

9. Type **Matt Gellman** and then press the **Tab** key. The value in the InvoiceAmt field is now highlighted.

10. Type **854** and then press the **Tab** key. Access changes the InvoiceAmt field value to $854.00, saves the record in the Order table, and moves the insertion point to the beginning of the third row. See Figure 2-19.

Figure 2-19	ORDER TABLE DATASHEET AFTER ENTERING THE SECOND RECORD

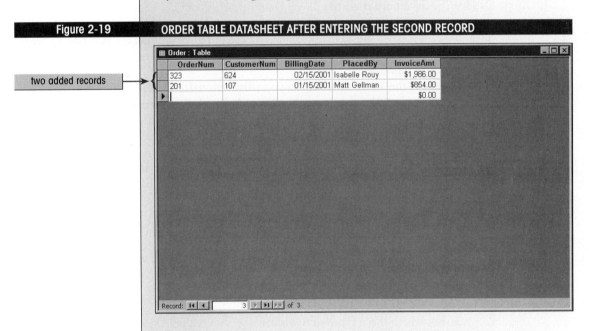

two added records

OrderNum	CustomerNum	BillingDate	PlacedBy	InvoiceAmt
323	624	02/15/2001	Isabelle Rouy	$1,986.00
201	107	01/15/2001	Matt Gellman	$854.00
				$0.00

Record: 14 4   3 ▶ ▶I ▶* of 3

Notice that "Record 3 of 3" appears around the navigation buttons, even though the table contains only two records. Access is anticipating that you will enter a new record, which would be the third of three records in the table. If you moved the insertion point to the second record, the display would change to "Record 2 of 2."

Even though the Order table contains only two records, Barbara asks you to print the table datasheet so that she can bring it with her to a staff meeting. She wants to show the table design to her staff members to make sure that it will meet their needs for tracking order data.

You'll use the Print button on the Table Datasheet toolbar to print one copy of the Order table with the current settings.

> ### To print the Order table:
>
> 1. Click the **Print** button 🖨 on the Table Datasheet toolbar.
>
> Notice that the two records are currently listed in the order in which you entered them. However, once you close the table or change to another view, and then redisplay the table datasheet, the records will be listed in primary key order by the values in the OrderNum field.

You have created the Order table in the Restaurant database and added two records to the table, which Access saved automatically to the database on your Data Disk.

Saving a Database

Notice the Save button on the Table Datasheet toolbar. This Save button, unlike the Save buttons in other Windows programs, does not save the active document (database) to your disk. Instead, you use the Save button to save the design of a table, query, form, or report, or to save datasheet format changes. Access does not have a button or option you can use to save the active database.

Access saves the active database to your disk automatically, both on a periodic basis and whenever you close the database. This means that if your database is stored on a disk in drive A, you should never remove the disk while the database file is open. If you do remove the disk, Access will encounter problems when it tries to save the database, which might damage the database.

The Order table is now complete. In Session 2.2, you'll continue to work with the Order table by modifying its structure and entering and maintaining data in the table.

Session 2.1 QUICK CHECK

1. What guidelines should you follow when you design a database?

2. What is the purpose of the data type property for a field?

3. For which three types of fields can you assign a field size?

4. Why did you define the OrderNum field as a text field instead of a number field?

5. A(n) _____ value, which results when you do not enter a value for a field, is not permitted for a primary key.

6. What does a pencil symbol in a datasheet's row selector represent? A star symbol?

SESSION 2.2

In this session, you will modify the structure of a table by deleting, moving, and adding fields and changing field properties; copy records from another Access database; and update a database by deleting and changing records.

Modifying the Structure of an Access Table

Even a well-designed table might need to be modified. For example, the government at all levels and the competition place demands on a company to track more data and to modify the data it already tracks. Access allows you to modify a table's structure in Design view: you can add and delete fields, change the order of fields, and change the properties of the fields.

After meeting with her staff members and reviewing the structure of the Order table and the format of the field values in the datasheet, Barbara has several changes she wants you to make to the table. First, she has decided that it's not necessary to keep track of the name of the person who placed a particular order, so she wants you to delete the PlacedBy field. Also, she thinks that the InvoiceAmt field should remain a currency field, but she wants the dollar signs removed from the displayed field values in the datasheet. She also wants the BillingDate field moved to the end of the table. Finally, she wants you to add a yes/no field, named Paid, to the table to indicate whether or not the customer has paid for the order. The Paid field will be inserted between the CustomerNum and InvoiceAmt fields. Figure 2-20 shows Barbara's modified design for the Order table.

Figure 2-20	MODIFIED DESIGN FOR THE ORDER TABLE			
Field Name	Data Type	Field Size	Description	
OrderNum	Text	3	primary key	
CustomerNum	Text	3	foreign key	
Paid	Yes/No			
InvoiceAmt	Currency			
BillingDate	Date/Time			

You'll begin modifying the table by deleting the PlacedBy field.

Deleting a Field

After you've defined a table structure and added records to the table, you can delete a field from the table structure. When you delete a field, you also delete all the values for the field from the table. Therefore, you should make sure that you need to delete a field and that you delete the correct field.

REFERENCE WINDOW   **RW**

Deleting a Field from a Table Structure
- In the Table window in Design view, right-click the row selector for the field you want to delete, to select the field and display the shortcut menu.
- Click Delete Rows on the shortcut menu.

You need to delete the PlacedBy field from the Order table structure.

To delete the PlacedBy field:

1. If you took a break after the previous session, make sure that Access is running and that the Order table of the Restaurant database is open.

2. Click the **View** button for Design view 🔲 on the Table Datasheet toolbar. The Table window for the Order table opens in Design view.

3. Position the pointer on the row selector for the PlacedBy field until the pointer changes to ➡.

4. Right-click to select the entire row for the field and display the shortcut menu, and then click **Delete Rows**.

   A dialog box opens asking you to confirm the deletion.

5. Click the **Yes** button to close the dialog box and to delete the field and its values from the table. See Figure 2-21.

Figure 2-21	TABLE STRUCTURE AFTER DELETING PLACEDBY FIELD

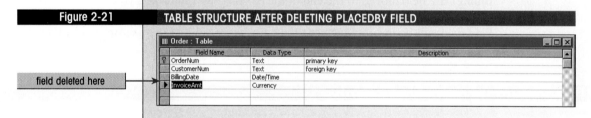

field deleted here

You have deleted the PlacedBy field in the Table window, but the change doesn't take place in the table on disk until you save the table structure. Because you have other modifications to make to the table, you'll wait until you finish them all before saving the modified table structure to disk.

Moving a Field

To move a field, you use the mouse to drag it to a new location in the Table window in Design view. Your next modification to the Order table structure is to move the BillingDate field to the end of the table, as Barbara requested.

To move the BillingDate field:

1. Click the **row selector** for the BillingDate field to select the entire row.

2. Place the pointer in the row selector for the BillingDate field, click the pointer ↳, and then drag the pointer ↳ to the row selector below the InvoiceAmt row selector. See Figure 2-22.

Figure 2-22	MOVING A FIELD IN THE TABLE STRUCTURE

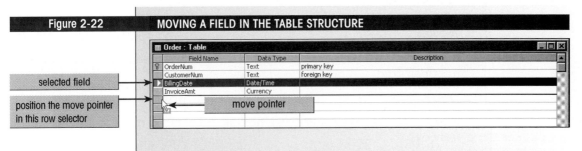

3. Release the mouse button. Access moves the BillingDate field below the InvoiceAmt field in the table structure.

TROUBLE? If the BillingDate field did not move, repeat Steps 1 through 3, making sure you firmly hold down the mouse button during the drag operation.

Adding a Field

Next, you need to add the Paid field to the table structure between the CustomerNum and InvoiceAmt fields. To add a new field between existing fields, you must insert a row. You begin by selecting the field that will be below the new field you want to insert.

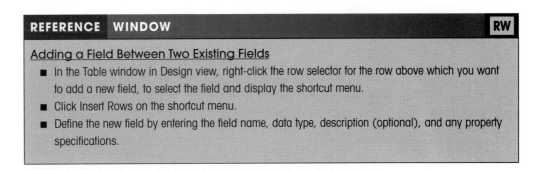

REFERENCE WINDOW **RW**

Adding a Field Between Two Existing Fields
- In the Table window in Design view, right-click the row selector for the row above which you want to add a new field, to select the field and display the shortcut menu.
- Click Insert Rows on the shortcut menu.
- Define the new field by entering the field name, data type, description (optional), and any property specifications.

To add the Paid field to the Order table:

1. Right-click the **row selector** for the InvoiceAmt field to select this field and display the shortcut menu, and then click **Insert Rows**. Access adds a new, blank row between the CustomerNum and InvoiceAmt fields. See Figure 2-23.

Figure 2-23	AFTER INSERTING A ROW IN THE TABLE STRUCTURE

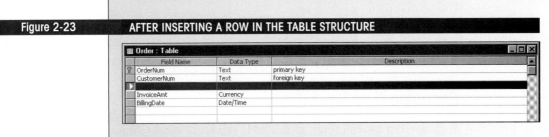

You'll define the Paid field in the new row for the Order table. Access will add this new field to the Order table structure between the CustomerNum and InvoiceAmt fields.

2. Click the **Field Name** text box for the new row, type **Paid**, and then press the **Tab** key.

The Paid field will be a yes/no field that will specify whether or not an invoice has been paid.

3. Type **y**. Access completes the data type as "yes/No."

4. Press the **Tab** key to select the yes/no data type and to move to the Description text box.

Notice that Access changes the value in the Data Type text box from "yes/No" to "Yes/No." Barbara wants the Paid field to have a Default Value property value of "No," so you need to set this property.

5. In the Field Properties section, click the **Default Value** text box, type **no**, and then click the **Description** text box for the Paid field. Notice that Access changes the Default Value property value from "no" to "No." See Figure 2-24.

Figure 2-24	PAID FIELD ADDED TO THE ORDER TABLE

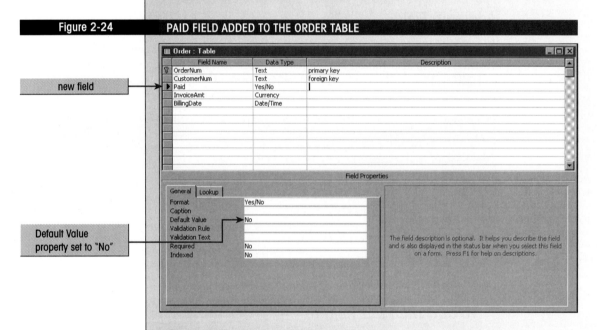

new field

Default Value
property set to "No"

Because its field name clearly indicates its purpose, you do not need to enter a description for the Paid field.

You've completed adding the Paid field to the Order table in Design view. As with the other changes you've made, however, the Paid field is not added to the Order table in the Restaurant database until you save the changes to the table structure.

Changing Field Properties

Barbara's last modification to the table structure is to remove the dollar signs from the InvoiceAmt field values displayed in the datasheet—repeated dollar signs are unnecessary and they clutter the datasheet. As you learned earlier when defining the BillingDate field, you use the Format property to control the display of a field value.

To change the Format property of the InvoiceAmt field:

1. Click the **Description** text box for the InvoiceAmt field. The InvoiceAmt field is now the current field.

2. Click the right side of the **Format** text box to display the Format list box. See Figure 2-25.

Figure 2-25	FORMAT LIST BOX

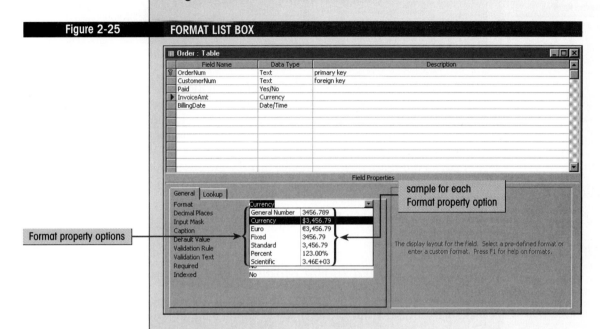

To the right of each Format property option is a field value whose appearance represents a sample of the option. The Standard option specifies the format Barbara wants for the InvoiceAmt field.

3. Click **Standard** in the Format list box to accept this option for the Format property.

Barbara wants you to add a third record to the Order table datasheet. Before you can add the record, you must save the modified table structure, and then switch to the Order table datasheet.

To save the modified table structure, and then switch to the datasheet:

1. Click the **Save** button ![save] on the Table Design toolbar. The modified table structure for the Order table is stored in the Restaurant database.

2. Click the **View** button for Datasheet view ![view] on the Table Design toolbar. The Order table datasheet opens. See Figure 2-26.

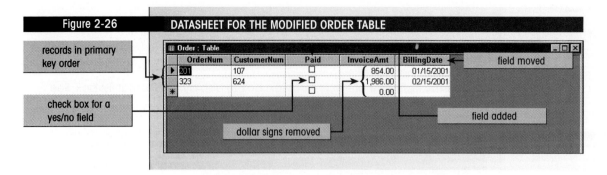

| Figure 2-26 | DATASHEET FOR THE MODIFIED ORDER TABLE |

Notice that the PlacedBy field no longer appears in the datasheet, the BillingDate field is now the rightmost column, the InvoiceAmt field values do not contain dollar signs, and the Paid field appears between the CustomerNum and InvoiceAmt fields. The Paid column contains check boxes to represent the yes/no field values. Empty check boxes signify "No," which is the default value you assigned to the Paid field. A "Yes" value is indicated by a check mark in the check box. Also notice that the records appear in ascending order based on the value in the OrderNum field, the Order table's primary key, even though you did not enter the records in this order.

Barbara asks you to add a third record to the table. This record is for an order that has been paid.

To add the record to the modified Order table:

1. Click the **New Record** button on the Table Datasheet toolbar. The insertion point is located in the OrderNum field for the third row, which is the next row available for a new record.

2. Type **211**. The pencil symbol appears in the row selector for the third row, and the star appears in the row selector for the fourth row. Recall that these symbols represent a record being edited and the next available record, respectively.

3. Press the **Tab** key. The insertion point moves to the CustomerNum field.

4. Type **201** and then press the **Tab** key. The Paid field is now the current field.

   Recall that the default value for this field is "No," which means the check box is initially empty. For yes/no fields with check boxes, you press the Tab key to leave the check box unchecked; you press the spacebar or click the check box to add or remove a check mark in the check box. Because the invoice for this order has been paid, you need to insert a check mark in the check box.

5. Press the **spacebar**. A check mark appears in the check box.

6. Press the **Tab** key. The value in the InvoiceAmt field is now highlighted.

7. Type **703.5** and then press the **Tab** key. The insertion point moves to the BillingDate field.

8. Type **01/15/01** and then press the **Tab** key. Access saves the record in the Order table and moves the insertion point to the beginning of the fourth row. See Figure 2-27.

Figure 2-27	ORDER TABLE DATASHEET WITH THIRD RECORD ADDED

"Yes" value

record added

OrderNum	CustomerNum	Paid	InvoiceAmt	BillingDate
201	107	☐	854.00	01/15/2001
323	624	☐	1,986.00	02/15/2001
211	201	☑	703.50	01/15/2001
		☐	0.00	

"No" values

As you add records, Access places them at the end of the datasheet. If you switch to Design view, then return to the datasheet, or if you close the table and then open the datasheet, Access will display the records in primary key sequence.

You have modified the Order table structure and added one record. Instead of typing the remaining records in the Order table, Barbara suggests that you copy them from a table that already exists in another database, and then paste them into the Order table.

Copying Records from Another Access Database

You can copy and paste records from a table in the same database or in a different database only if the tables have the same structure—that is, the tables contain the same fields in the same order. Barbara's Valle database in the Tutorial folder on your Data Disk has a table named Restaurant Order that has the same table structure as the Order table. The records in the Restaurant Order table are the records Barbara wants you to copy into the Order table.

Other programs, such as Microsoft Word and Microsoft Excel, allow you to have two or more documents open at a time. However, you can have only one Access database open at a time. Therefore, you need to close the Restaurant database, open the Restaurant Order table in the Valle database, select and copy the table records, close the Valle database, reopen the Order table in the Restaurant database, and then paste the copied records.

To copy the records from the Restaurant Order table:

1. Click the **Close** button ☒ on the Table window title bar to close the Order table, and then click the **Close** button ☒ on the Database window title bar to close the Restaurant database.

2. Click the **Open** button 🖆 on the Database toolbar to display the Open dialog box.

3. If necessary, display the list of files on your Data Disk, and then open the **Tutorial** folder.

4. Open the database file named **Valle**. The Database window opens, showing the tables for the Valle database.

   Notice that the Valle database contains two tables: the Restaurant Customer table and the Restaurant Order table. The Restaurant Order table contains the records you need to copy.

5. Click **Restaurant Order** in the Tables list box, and then click the **Open** button in the Database window. The datasheet for the Restaurant Order table opens. See Figure 2-28. Note that this table contains a total of 102 records.

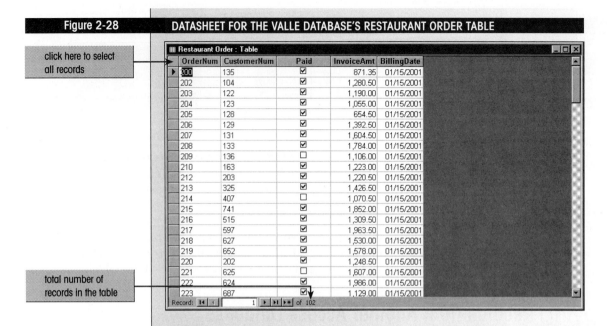

Figure 2-28   DATASHEET FOR THE VALLE DATABASE'S RESTAURANT ORDER TABLE

click here to select all records

total number of records in the table

Barbara wants you to copy all the records in the Restaurant Order table. You can select all records by clicking the row selector for the field name row.

6. Click the **row selector** for the field name row (see Figure 2-28). All the records in the table are now highlighted, which means that Access has selected all of them.

7. Click the **Copy** button 📋 on the Table Datasheet toolbar. All of the records are copied to the Windows Clipboard.

   TROUBLE? If a Clipboard toolbar opens, click its Close button to close it, and then continue with Step 8.

8. Click the **Close** button ⊠ on the Table window title bar. A dialog box opens asking if you want to save the data you copied on the Windows Clipboard.

9. Click the **Yes** button in the dialog box. The dialog box closes, and then the table closes.

10. Click the **Close** button ⊠ on the Database window title bar to close the Valle database.

To finish copying and pasting the records, you must open the Order table and paste the copied records into the table.

To paste the copied records into the Order table:

1. Click **File** on the menu bar, and then click **Restaurant** in the list of recently opened databases. The Database window opens, showing the tables for the Restaurant database.

2. In the Tables list box, click **Order** (if necessary) and then click the **Open** button in the Database window. The datasheet for the Order table opens.

   You must paste the records at the end of the table.

3. Click the **row selector** for row four, which is the next row available for a new record.

4. Click the **Paste** button 📋 on the Table Datasheet toolbar. A dialog box opens, asking if you are sure you want to paste the records (102 in all).

5. Click the **Yes** button. All the records are pasted from the Windows Clipboard, and the pasted records remain highlighted. See Figure 2-29. Notice that the table now contains a total of 105 records—the three original records plus the 102 copied records.

Figure 2-29	TABLE AFTER COPYING AND PASTING RECORDS

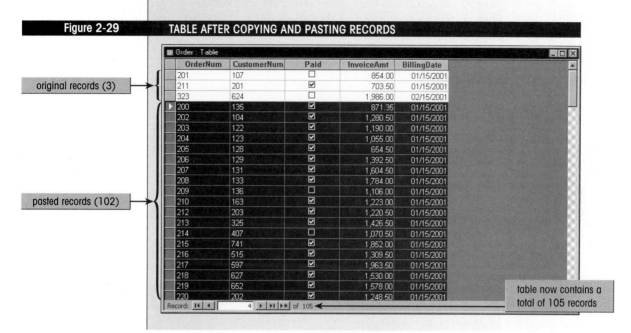

original records (3)

pasted records (102)

table now contains a total of 105 records

Using the Office Clipboard

When you copied records from the Valle database and pasted them into the Restaurant database, you used the Windows Clipboard. The **Windows Clipboard** is a temporary storage area for data that is cut or copied to it from any Windows program. The data is stored on the Clipboard until you either close Windows or cut or copy something else to the Clipboard.

When you need to copy multiple pieces of data from one program to another—or within the same program (such as Access)—you can use the Office Clipboard. The **Office Clipboard** lets you cut or copy up to 12 different items from any Office 2000 program so that you can paste these items into different locations later. For example, if you need to copy the records from Barbara's Valle database, and then open another database and copy additional records from it, you could copy each set of records to the Office Clipboard, open the Restaurant database, and then paste these two different sets of records in two actions. If you used the Windows Clipboard to copy the same records, you would only be able to paste the records from the second database, because the first set of records would be replaced by the second set of records when you performed the second copy operation.

The Office Clipboard appears automatically as a Clipboard toolbar as soon as you cut or copy two items to it. When the Clipboard toolbar opens, you will see a Copy button, Paste All button, and a Clear Clipboard button, along with icons that represent each item that you either cut or copied to the Clipboard. To paste an item in a new location, such as pasting records copied from one table to another, you select the location in which to paste the item, and then click the icon that contains the data to paste. In Access, the Paste All button is not available all the time, but you can still paste groups of items by inserting them individually.

You've completed copying and pasting the records between the two tables. Now that you have all the records in the Order table, Barbara examines the records to make sure they are correct. She finds one record that she wants you to delete and another record that needs changes to its field values.

Updating a Database

Updating, or **maintaining**, a database is the process of adding, changing, and deleting records in database tables to keep them current and accurate. You've already added records to the Order table. Now Barbara wants you to delete and change records.

Deleting Records

To delete a record, you need to select the record in Datasheet view, and then delete it using the Delete Record button on the Table Datasheet toolbar or the Delete Record option on the shortcut menu.

> **REFERENCE WINDOW**   **RW**
>
> Deleting a Record
> - In the Table window in Datasheet view, click the row selector for the record you want to delete, and then click the Delete Record button on the Table Datasheet toolbar (or right-click the row selector for the record, and then click Delete Record on the shortcut menu).
> - In the dialog box asking you to confirm the deletion, click the Yes button.

Barbara asks you to delete the record whose OrderNum is 200 because this record was entered in error; it represents an order from an office customer, not a restaurant customer, and therefore does not belong in the Restaurant database. The fourth record in the table has an OrderNum value of 200. This record is the one you need to delete.

To delete the record:

1. Right-click the **row selector** for row four. Access selects the fourth record and displays the shortcut menu. See Figure 2-30.

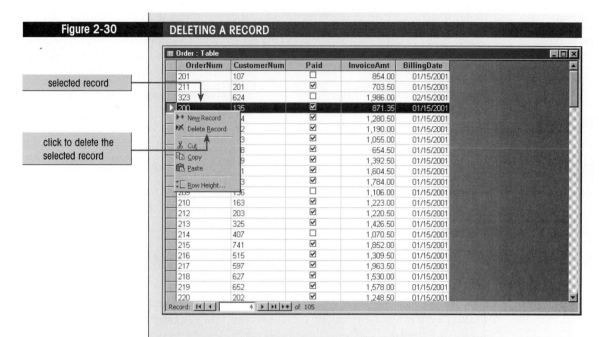

Figure 2-30   DELETING A RECORD

selected record

click to delete the
selected record

2. Click **Delete Record** on the shortcut menu. Access deletes the record and opens a dialog box asking you to confirm the deletion.

TROUBLE? If you selected the wrong record for deletion, click the No button. Access ends the deletion process and redisplays the deleted record. Repeat Steps 1 and 2 to delete the correct record.

3. Click the **Yes** button to confirm the deletion and close the dialog box.

Barbara's final update to the Order table involves changes to field values in one of the records.

Changing Records

To change the field values in a record, you first must make the record the current record. Then you position the insertion point in the field value to make minor changes or select the field value to replace it entirely. In Tutorial 1, you used the mouse with the scroll bars and the navigation buttons to navigate through the records in a datasheet. You can also use keystroke combinations and the F2 key to navigate a datasheet and to select field values.

The **F2 key** is a toggle that you use to switch between navigation mode and editing mode:

- In **navigation mode**, Access selects an entire field value. If you type while you are in navigation mode, your typed entry replaces the highlighted field value.

- In **editing mode**, you can insert or delete characters in a field value based on the location of the insertion point.

Figure 2-31 shows some of the navigation mode and editing mode keystroke techniques.

Figure 2-31	NAVIGATION MODE AND EDITING MODE KEYSTROKE TECHNIQUES	
PRESS	**TO MOVE THE SELECTION IN NAVIGATION MODE**	**TO MOVE THE INSERTION POINT IN EDITING MODE**
←	Left one field value at a time	Left one character at a time
→	Right one field value at a time	Right one character at a time
Home	Left to the first field value in the record	To the left of the first character in the field value
End	Right to the last field value in the record	To the right of the last character in the field value
↑ or ↓	Up or down one record at a time	Up or down one record at a time and switch to navigation mode
Tab or Enter	Right one field value at a time	Right one field value at a time and switch to navigation mode
Ctrl + Home	To the first field value in the first record	To the left of the first character in the field value
Ctrl + End	To the last field value in the last record	To the right of the last character in the field value

The record Barbara wants you to change has an OrderNum field value of 397. Some of the values were entered incorrectly for this record, and you need to enter the correct values.

To modify the record:

1. Make sure the OrderNum field value for the fourth record is still highlighted, indicating that the table is in navigation mode.

2. Press **Ctrl + End**. Access displays records from the end of the table and selects the last field value in the last record. This field value is for the BillingDate field.

3. Press the **Home** key. The first field value in the last record is now selected. This field value is for the OrderNum field.

4. Press the **↑** key. The OrderNum field value for the previous record is selected. This record is the one you need to change.

   Barbara wants you to change these field values in the record: OrderNum to 398, CustomerNum to 165, Paid to "Yes" (checked), and InvoiceAmt to 1426.50. You do not need to change the BillingDate.

5. Type **398**, press the **Tab** key, type **165**, press the **Tab** key, press the **spacebar** to insert a check mark in the Paid check box, press the **Tab** key, and then type **1426.5**. The changes to the record are complete.

6. Press the **↓** key to save the changes to the record and make the next record the current record. See Figure 2-32.

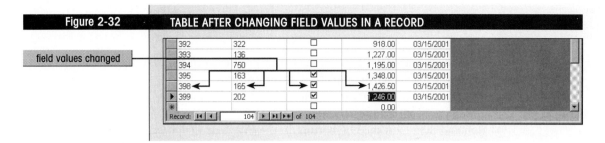

| Figure 2-32 | TABLE AFTER CHANGING FIELD VALUES IN A RECORD |

field values changed

392	322	☐	918.00	03/15/2001
393	136	☐	1,227.00	03/15/2001
394	750	☐	1,195.00	03/15/2001
395	163	☑	1,348.00	03/15/2001
398	165	☑	1,426.50	03/15/2001
399	202	☑	1,246.00	03/15/2001
*		☐	0.00	

Record: 14 ◄ | 104 | ► ►I ►* of 104

You've completed all of Barbara's updates to the Order table. Barbara asks you to print only the first page of data from the Order table datasheet so that she can show the revised table structure to her staff members. After you print the page, you can exit Access.

To print the first page of Order table data, and then exit Access:

1. Click **File** on the menu bar, and then click **Print** to open the Print dialog box.

2. In the Print Range section, click the **Pages** option button, type **1** in the From text box, press the **Tab** key, and then type **1** in the To text box.

3. Click the **OK** button to print the first page of data.

   Now you can exit Access.

4. Click the **Close** button ☒ on the Access window title bar to close the Order table and the Restaurant database and to exit Access.

Barbara and her staff members approve of the revised table structure for the Order table. They are confident that the table will allow them to easily track order data for Valle Coffee's restaurant customers.

Session 2.2 QUICK CHECK

1. What is the effect of deleting a field from a table structure?

2. How do you insert a field between existing fields in a table structure?

3. A field with the _____ data type can appear in the table datasheet as a check box.

4. Which property do you use to control the display appearance of a field value?

5. Why must you close an open database when you want to copy records to it from a table in another database?

6. What is the difference between navigation mode and editing mode?

REVIEW ASSIGNMENTS

Barbara needs a database to track the coffee products offered by Valle Coffee. She asks you to create the database by completing the following:

1. Make sure your Data Disk is in the disk drive, and then start Access.

Explore 2. In the initial Microsoft Access dialog box, click the Blank Access database option button, and then click the OK button. In the File New Database dialog box, select the Review folder on your Data Disk, and then enter the name **Valle Products** for the database in the File name text box. Click the Create button to create the new database.

Explore 3. Display the Table window in Design view (if necessary), and then create a table using the table design shown in Figure 2-33.

Figure 2-33

Field Name	Data Type	Description	Field Size	Other Properties
ProductCode	Text	primary key	4	
CoffeeCode	Text	foreign key	4	
Price	Currency	price for this product		Format: Fixed
				Decimal Places: 2
Decaf	Text	D if decaf, Null if regular	1	Default Value: D
BackOrdered	Yes/No	back-ordered from supplier?		

4. Specify ProductCode as the primary key, and then save the table as **Product**.
5. Add the product records shown in Figure 2-34 to the **Product** table. (*Hint*: You must type the decimal point when entering the Price field values.)

Figure 2-34

ProductCode	CoffeeCode	Price	Decaf	BackOrdered
2316	JRUM	8.99		Yes
9754	HAZL	40.00	D	Yes
9309	COCO	9.99	D	No

6. Make the following changes to the structure of the **Product** table:
   a. Add a new field between the CoffeeCode and Price fields, using these properties:
      Field Name: WeightCode
      Data Type: Text
      Description: foreign key
      Field Size: 1
   b. Move the Decaf field so that it appears between the WeightCode and Price fields.
   c. Save the revised table structure.
7. Use the **Product** datasheet to update the database as follows:
   a. Enter these WeightCode values for the three records: A for ProductCode 2316, A for ProductCode 9309, and E for ProductCode 9754.
   b. Add a record to the **Product** datasheet with these field values:
      ProductCode: 9729
      CoffeeCode: COLS
      WeightCode: E
      Decaf: D
      Price: 39.75
      BackOrdered: Yes
8. Close the **Product** table, and then set the option for compacting the **Valle Products** database on close.

9. Barbara created a database with her name as the database name. The **Coffee Product** table in that database has the same format as the **Product** table you created. Copy all the records from the **Coffee Product** table in the **Barbara** database (located in the Review folder on your Data Disk) to the end of your **Product** table.

Explore 10. Because you added a number of records to the database, its size has increased. Compact the database manually using the Compact and Repair Database option.

11. Reopen the **Product** datasheet. The records now appear in primary key order by ProductCode. Then delete the record with the ProductCode 2372 from the **Product** table.

12. Delete the BackOrdered field from the **Product** table structure.

Explore 13. Use the Access Help system to learn how to resize datasheet columns to fit the data, and then resize all columns in the datasheet for the **Product** table so that each column fits its data. Scroll the datasheet to make sure all field values are fully displayed. For any field values that are not fully displayed, make sure the field values are visible on the screen, and then resize the appropriate columns again.

14. Print the first page of data from the **Product** table datasheet, and then save and close the table.

Explore 15. Create a table named **Weight**, based on the data shown in Figure 2-35, according to the following steps:

Figure 2-35

WeightCode	Weight/Size
A	1 lb pkg
B	6 lb case
C	24 ct 1.5 oz pkg
D	44 ct 1.25 oz pkg
E	44 ct 1.5 oz pkg
F	88 ct 1.25 oz pkg
G	88 ct 1.5 oz pkg

a. Select the Datasheet View option in the New Table dialog box.

b. Enter the seven records shown in Figure 2-35. (Do *not* enter the field names at this point.)

c. Switch to Design view, supply the table name, and then answer No if asked if you want to create a primary key.

d. Type the following field names and set the following properties:

WeightCode
Description: primary key
Field Size: 1
Weight/Size
Description: weight in pounds or size in packages (number and weight) per case
Field Size: 17

e. Specify the primary key, save the table structure changes, and then switch back to Datasheet view. If you receive any warning messages, answer Yes to continue.

f. Resize both datasheet columns to fit the data (use Access Help to learn how to resize datasheet columns, if necessary); then save, print, and close the datasheet.

Explore 16. Create a table named **Coffee** using the Import Table Wizard, which is available in the New Table dialog box. The table you need to import is named **Coffee.dbf** and is located in the Review folder on your Data Disk. This table has a dBASE 5 file type. (You'll need to change the entry in the Files of type list box to display the file in the list.) After importing the table, complete the following:

a. Change all field names to use the Valle Coffee convention of uppercase and lowercase letters, and then enter the following Description property values:

CoffeeCode: primary key
Decaf: is this coffee available in decaf?

b. Change the Format property of the Decaf field to Yes/No.

c. Specify the primary key, and then save the table structure changes.

d. Switch to Datasheet view, and then resize all columns in the datasheet to fit the data. (Use Access Help to learn how to resize datasheet columns, if necessary.) Be sure to scroll through the table to make sure that all field values are fully displayed.

e. Save, print, and then close the datasheet.

17. Close the **Valle Products** database, and then exit Access.

CASE PROBLEMS

Case 1. Ashbrook Mall Information Desk Sam Bullard, the director of the Mall Operations Office at Ashbrook Mall, uses the **MallJobs** database to maintain information about current job openings at stores in the mall. Sam asks you to help him maintain the database by completing the following:

1. Make sure your Data Disk is in the disk drive.

2. Start Access and open the **MallJobs** database located in the Cases folder on your Data Disk.

3. Create a table using the table design shown in Figure 2-36.

Figure 2-36

Field Name	Data Type	Description	Field Size
Job	Text	primary key	5
Store	Text	foreign key	3
Hours/Week	Text		20
Position	Text		35
ExperienceReq	Yes/No		

4. Specify Job as the primary key, and then save the table as **Job**.

5. Add the job records shown in Figure 2-37 to the **Job** table.

Figure 2-37

Job	Store	Hours/Week	Position	ExperienceReq
10037	TH	negotiable	Salesclerk	Yes
10053	BR	16-32	Server	No
10022	BE	35-45	Assistant Manager	Yes

6. Sam created a database named **Openings** that contains a table with job data named **Current Jobs**. The **Job** table you created has the same format as the **Current Jobs** table. Copy all the records from the **Current Jobs** table in the **Openings** database (located in the Cases folder on your Data Disk) to the end of your **Job** table.

7. Modify the structure of the **Job** table by completing the following:

a. Delete the ExperienceReq field.

b. Move the Hours/Week field so that it follows the Position field.

Explore 8. Use the Access Help system to learn how to resize datasheet columns to fit the data, and then switch to Datasheet view and resize all columns in the datasheet for the **Job** table.

9. Use the Job datasheet to update the database as follows:
   a. For Job 10048, change the Position value to Clerk, and change the Hours/Week value to 25-35.
   b. Add a record to the **Job** datasheet with the following field values:

Job:	10034
Store:	JB
Position:	Salesclerk
Hours/Week:	negotiable

   c. Delete the record for Job 10031.
10. Switch to Design view, and then switch back to Datasheet view so that the records appear in primary key sequence by Job.
11. Print the **Job** table datasheet, and then save and close the table.
12. Close the **MallJobs** database, and then exit Access.

Case 2. Professional Litigation User Services (PLUS) Raj Jawahir is responsible for tracking the daily payments received from PLUS clients. You'll help him maintain the **Payments** database by completing the following:

1. Make sure your Data Disk is in the disk drive.
2. Start Access and open the **Payments** database located in the Cases folder on your Data Disk.

> **Explore**

3. Create a table named **Payment** using the table design shown in Figure 2-38. (*Hint:* Make sure that you include spaces between the components of the custom format for the DatePaid field.)

Figure 2-38

Field Name	Data Type	Description	Field Size	Other Properties
Payment#	Text	primary key	5	
Firm#	Text	foreign key	4	
DatePaid	Date/Time			Format: mmm dd yyyy (custom format)
AmtPaid	Currency			Format: Standard

4. Add the payment records shown in Figure 2-39 to the **Payment** table.

Figure 2-39

Payment#	Firm#	DatePaid	AmtPaid
10031	1111	06/03/2001	2500.00
10002	1147	06/01/2001	1700.00
10015	1151	06/02/2001	2000.00

5. Modify the structure of the **Payment** table by completing the following:
   a. Add a new field between the Payment# and Firm# fields, using these properties:

Field Name:	Deposit#
Data Type:	Text
Field Size:	3

   b. Move the DatePaid field so that it follows the AmtPaid field.
6. Use the **Payment** datasheet to update the database as follows:
   a. Enter these Deposit# values for the three records: 101 for Payment# 10002, 102 for Payment# 10015, and 103 for Payment# 10031.
   b. Add a record to the **Payment** datasheet with these field values:

Payment#:	10105
Deposit#:	117
Firm#:	1103
AmtPaid:	1,750.00
DatePaid:	06/20/2001

7. Raj created a database named **PlusPays** that contains recent payments in the **Payment Records** table. The **Payment** table you created has the same format as the **Payment Records** table. Copy all the records from the **Payment Records** table in the **PlusPays** database (located in the Cases folder on your Data Disk) to the end of your **Payment** table.

Explore ▶ 8. Use the Access Help system to learn how to resize datasheet columns to fit the data, and then resize all columns in the datasheet for the **Payment** table.

9. For Payment# 10002, change the AmtPaid value to 1300.00.

10. Delete the record for Payment# 10096.

11. Print the first page of data from the **Payment** table datasheet, and then save and close the table.

12. Close the **Payments** database, and then exit Access.

Case 3. Best Friends Noah and Sheila Warnick continue to track information about participants in the walk-a-thons held to benefit Best Friends. Help them maintain the **Walks** database by completing the following:

1. Make sure your Data Disk is in the disk drive.

2. Start Access and open the **Walks** database located in the Cases folder on your Data Disk.

Explore ▶ 3. Create a table named **Pledge** using the Import Table Wizard. The table you need to import is named **Pledge.db** and is located in the Cases folder on your Data Disk. This table has a Paradox file type. (You'll need to change the entry in the Files of type list box to display the file in the list.) After importing the table, complete the following:

   a. Change all field names to use uppercase and lowercase letters, as appropriate, and then enter the following Description property values:

      PledgeNo: primary key

      WalkerID: foreign key

      PerMile: amount pledged per mile

   b. Specify the primary key, and then save the table structure changes.

   c. Switch to Datasheet view, and then resize all columns in the datasheet to fit the data. (Use Access Help to learn how to resize datasheet columns, if necessary.)

Explore ▶ 4. Modify the structure of the **Pledge** table by completing the following:

   a. Add a new field between the PaidAmt and PerMile fields, using these properties:

      Field Name: DatePaid

      Data Type: Date/Time

      Format: mm/dd/yyyy (custom format)

   b. Change the Data Type of both the PledgeAmt field and the PaidAmt field to Currency. For each of these fields, choose the Fixed format.

   c. Save the table structure. Answer Yes to any warning messages.

5. Use the **Pledge** datasheet to update the database as follows:

   a. Enter these DatePaid values for the five records: 09/15/2001 for PledgeNo 1, 09/01/2001 for PledgeNo 2, 08/25/2001 for PledgeNo 3, 09/20/2001 for PledgeNo 4, and 08/14/2001 for PledgeNo 5. Resize the DatePaid column to fit the data.

   b. Add a record to the **Pledge** datasheet with these field values:

      PledgeNo: 6

      Pledger: Gene Delsener

      WalkerID: 138

      PledgeAmt: 50

      PaidAmt: 50

      DatePaid: 09/18/2001

      PerMile: 0

   c. Enter the value 133 in the WalkerID field for PledgeNo 1.

   d. Change both the PledgeAmt value and the PaidAmt value for PledgeNo 3 to 25.00.

   e. Change the WalkerID value for PledgeNo 5 to 165.

6. Print the **Pledge** table datasheet, and then save and close the table.

7. Close the **Walks** database, and then exit Access.

Case 4. Lopez Lexus Dealerships   Maria and Hector Lopez use the **Lexus** database to track the car inventory in the chain of Lexus dealerships they own. You'll help them maintain the **Lexus** database by completing the following:

1. Make sure your Data Disk is in the disk drive.
2. Start Access and open the **Lexus** database located in the Cases folder on your Data Disk.

Explore   3. Use the Import Spreadsheet Wizard to create a new table named **Locations**. The data you need to import is contained in the **Lopez** workbook, which is a Microsoft Excel file located in the Cases folder on your Data Disk.
   a. Select the Import Table option in the New Table dialog box.
   b. Change the entry in the Files of type list box to display the list of Excel workbook files in the Cases folder.
   c. Select the **Lopez** file and then click the Import button.
   d. In the Import Spreadsheet Wizard dialog boxes, choose the option for using column headings as field names; select the option for choosing your own primary key, and specify LocationCode as the primary key; and enter the table name (**Locations**). Otherwise, accept the Wizard's choices for all other options for the imported data.

Explore   4. Use the Access Help system to learn how to resize datasheet columns to fit the data, and then open the **Locations** table and resize all columns in the datasheet.

5. Modify the structure of the **Locations** table by completing the following:
   a. For the LocationCode field, enter a Description property of "primary key," change the Field Size to 2, and change the Required property to Yes.
   b. For the LocationName field, change the Field Size to 25.
   c. For the ManagerName field, change the Field Size to 35.
   d. Save the table. If you receive any warning messages about lost data or integrity rules, click the Yes button.

6. Use the **Locations** datasheet to update the database as follows:
   a. For LocationCode A2, change the ManagerName value to Curran, Edward.
   b. Add a record to the **Locations** datasheet with these field values:
      LocationCode: H2
      LocationName: Houston
      ManagerName: Cohen, Molly
   c. Delete the record for LocationCode L2.

7. Print the **Locations** table datasheet, and then close the table.

Explore   8. Use the Table Wizard to create a new table named **Managers** based on the sample **Employees** table, which is a sample table in the Business category, as follows:
   a. Add the following sample fields to your table (in the following order): SocialSecurityNumber, LastName, Region, DateHired, and Salary. Do *not* click the Next button yet.
   b. Click LastName in the "Fields in my new table" list, click the Rename Field button in the first Table Wizard dialog box, and then change the LastName field name to ManagerName. Click the Next button.
   c. Change the default table name to **Managers**. Select the option to create your own primary key, and then select an appropriate field as your primary key. (*Hint:* Select a field that will contain unique numbers, and then select the correct option button that represents your data.) Click the Next button, and then click the Finish button in the final Table Wizard dialog box.

   d. Enter the following data into the **Managers** table:
      Social Security Number: 789-00-8642
      ManagerName: Evans, Hannah
      Region: Austin
      DateHired: 05/31/96
      Salary: 52,000
   e. Resize all columns in the datasheet to fit the data.

9. Print the **Managers** table datasheet, and then save and close the table.
10. Close the **Lexus** database, and then exit Access.

INTERNET ASSIGNMENTS

The purpose of the Internet Assignments is to challenge you to find information on the Internet that you can use to create effective documents. The actual assignments are updated and maintained on the Course Technology Web site. Log on to the Internet and use your Web browser to go to the Student Online Companion to accompany this text at **www.course.com/NewPerspectives/office2000**. Click the Access link, and then click the link for Tutorial 2.

QUICK | CHECK ANSWERS

Session 2.1

1. Identify all the fields needed to produce the required information, group related fields into tables, determine each table's primary key, include a common field in related tables, avoid data redundancy, and determine the properties of each field.
2. The data type determines what field values you can enter for the field and what other properties the field will have.
3. text, number, and AutoNumber fields
4. Order numbers will not be used for calculations.
5. null
6. the record being edited; the next row available for a new record

Session 2.2

1. The field and all its values are removed from the table.
2. In Design view, right-click the row selector for the row above which you want to insert the field, click Insert Rows on the shortcut menu, and then define the new field.
3. yes/no
4. Format property
5. Access allows you to have only one database open at a time.
6. In navigation mode, the entire field value is selected, and anything you type replaces the field value; in editing mode, you can insert or delete characters in a field value based on the location of the insertion point.

In this tutorial you will:

- Learn how to use the Query window in Design view

- Create, run, and save queries

- Define a relationship between two tables

- Sort data in a query

- Filter data in a query

- Specify an exact match condition in a query

- Change a datasheet's appearance

- Use a comparison operator to match a range of values

- Use the And and Or logical operators

- Perform calculations in a query using calculated fields, aggregate functions, and record group calculations

QUERYING A DATABASE

Retrieving Information About Restaurant Customers and Their Orders

CASE

Valle Coffee

At a recent company meeting, Leonard Valle and other Valle Coffee employees discussed the importance of regularly monitoring the business activity of the company's restaurant customers. For example, Kim Carpenter and her marketing staff track customer activity to develop new strategies for promoting Valle Coffee products. Barbara Hennessey and her office staff need to track information about all the orders for which bills were sent out on a specific date, so that they can determine whether the bills have been paid. In addition, Leonard is interested in analyzing the payment history of restaurant customers to determine which customers pay their invoices in a timely manner, which customers have higher invoice amounts, and so on. All of these informational needs can be satisfied by queries that retrieve information from the Restaurant database.

SESSION 3.1

In this session, you will use the Query window in Design view to create, run, and save queries; define a one-to-many relationship between two tables; sort data with a toolbar button and in Design view; and filter data in a query datasheet.

Introduction to Queries

As you learned in Tutorial 1, a query is a question you ask about data stored in a database. For example, Kim might create a query to find records in the Customer table for only those customers location in a specific state. When you create a query, you tell Access which fields you need and what criteria Access should use to select the records.

Access provides powerful query capabilities that allow you to:

- display selected fields and records from a table
- sort records
- perform calculations
- generate data for forms, reports, and other queries
- update data in the tables in a database
- find and display data from two or more tables

Most questions about data are generalized queries in which you specify the fields and records you want Access to select. These common requests for information, such as "Which customers have unpaid bills?" or "Which type of coffee sells best in Ohio?" are called **select queries**. The answer to a select query is returned in the form of a datasheet.

More specialized, technical queries, such as finding duplicate records in a table, are best formulated using a Query Wizard. A Query Wizard prompts you for information by asking a series of questions and then creates the appropriate query based on your answers. In Tutorial 1, you used the Simple Query Wizard to display only some of the fields in the Customer table; Access provides other Query Wizards for more complex queries. For common, informational queries, it is easier for you to design your own query than to use a Query Wizard.

Kim wants you to create a query to display the customer number, customer name, city, owner name, and first contact information for each record in the Customer table. She needs this information for a market analysis her staff is completing on Valle Coffee's restaurant customers. You'll open the Query window to create the query for Kim.

Query Window

You use the Query window in Design view to create a query. In Design view you specify the data you want to view by constructing a query by example. Using **query by example (QBE)**, you give Access an example of the information you are requesting. Access then retrieves the information that precisely matches your example.

For Kim's query, you need to display data from the Customer table. You'll begin by starting Access, opening the Restaurant database, and displaying the Query window in Design view.

> *To start Access, open the Restaurant database, and open the Query window in Design view:*
>
> 1. Place your Data Disk in the appropriate disk drive.
>
> 2. Start Access and open the **Restaurant** database located in the Tutorial folder on your Data Disk. The Restaurant database is displayed in the Database window.

3. Click **Queries** in the Objects bar of the Database window, and then click the **New** button. The New Query dialog box opens. See Figure 3-1.

| Figure 3-1 | NEW QUERY DIALOG BOX |

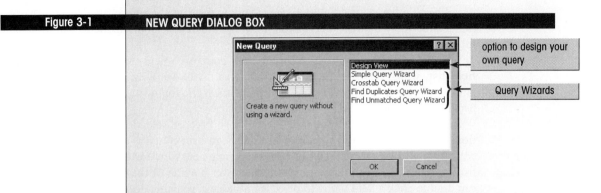

You'll design your own query instead of using a Query Wizard.

4. If necessary, click **Design View** in the list box.

5. Click the **OK** button. Access opens the Show Table dialog box on top of the Query window. (Note that you could also have double-clicked the option "Create query in Design view" from the Database window.) Notice that the title bar of the Query window shows that you are creating a select query.

The query you are creating will retrieve data from the Customer table, so you need to add this table to the Select Query window.

6. Click **Customer** in the Tables list box (if necessary), click the **Add** button, and then click the **Close** button. Access places the Customer table's field list in the Select Query window and closes the Show Table dialog box.

To display more of the fields you'll be using for creating queries, you'll maximize the Select Query window.

7. Click the **Maximize** button on the Select Query window title bar. See Figure 3-2.

| Figure 3-2 | SELECT QUERY WINDOW IN DESIGN VIEW |

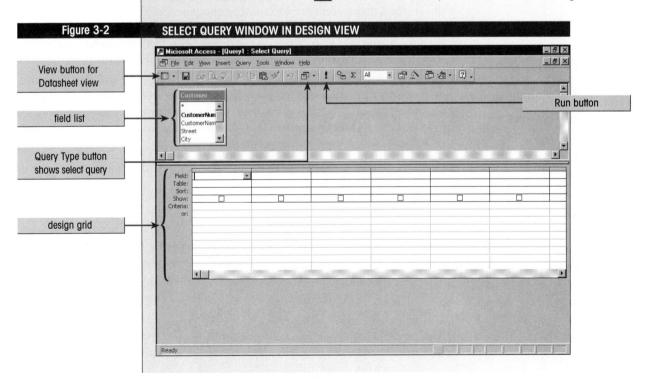

In Design view, the Select Query window contains the standard title bar, menu bar, status bar, and the Query Design toolbar. On the toolbar, the Query Type button shows a select query; the icon on this button changes according to the type of query you are creating. The title bar on the Select Query window displays the query type, Select Query, and the default query name, Query1. You'll change the default query name to a more meaningful one later when you save the query.

The Select Query window in Design view contains a field list and the design grid. The **field list**, which appears in the upper-left area of the window, contains the fields for the table you are querying. The table name appears at the top of the list box, and the fields are listed in the order in which they appear in the table.

In the **design grid**, you include the fields and record selection criteria for the information you want to see. Each column in the design grid contains specifications about a field you will use in the query. You can choose a single field for your query by dragging its name from the field list to the design grid in the lower portion of the window. Alternatively, you can double-click a field name to place it in the next available design grid column.

When you are constructing a query, you can see the query results at any time by clicking the View button or the Run button on the Query Design toolbar. In response, Access displays the datasheet, which contains the set of fields and records that results from answering, or **running**, the query. The order of the fields in the datasheet is the same as the order of the fields in the design grid. Although the datasheet looks just like a table datasheet and appears in Datasheet view, a query datasheet is temporary, and its contents are based on the criteria you establish in the design grid. In contrast, a table datasheet shows the permanent data in a table. However, you can update data while viewing a query datasheet, just as you can when working in a table datasheet or a form.

If the query you are creating includes every field from the specified table, you can use one of the following three methods to transfer all the fields from the field list to the design grid:

■ Click and drag each field individually from the field list to the design grid. Use this method if you want the fields in your query to appear in an order that is different from the order in the field list.

■ Double-click the asterisk in the field list. Access places the table name followed by a period and an asterisk (as in "Customer.*") in the design grid, which signifies that the order of the fields will be the same in the query as it is in the field list. Use this method if you don't need to sort the query or specify conditions for the records you want to select. The advantage of using this method is that you do not need to change the query if you add or delete fields from the underlying table structure. Such changes are reflected automatically in the query.

■ Double-click the field list title bar to highlight all the fields, and then click and drag one of the highlighted fields to the design grid. Access places each field in a separate column and arranges the fields in the order in which they appear in the field list. Use this method rather than the previous one if you need to sort your query or include record selection criteria.

Now you'll create and run Kim's query to display selected fields from the Customer table.

Creating **and Running a Query**

The default table datasheet displays all the fields in the table, in the same order as they appear in the table. In contrast, a query datasheet can display selected fields from a table, and the order of the fields can be different from that of the table.

Kim wants the CustomerNum, CustomerName, City, OwnerName, and FirstContact fields to appear in the query results. You'll add each of these fields to the design grid.

To select the fields for the query, and then run the query:

1. Drag **CustomerNum** from the Customer field list to the design grid's first column Field text box, and then release the mouse button. See Figure 3-3.

Figure 3-3	FIELD ADDED TO THE DESIGN GRID

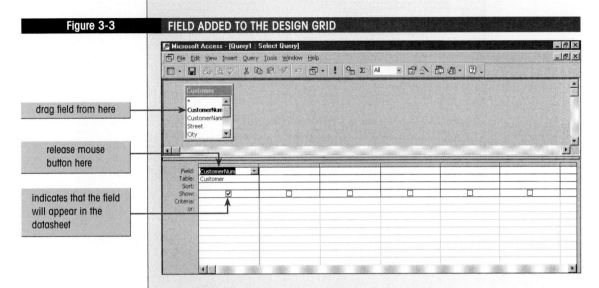

drag field from here

release mouse button here

indicates that the field will appear in the datasheet

In the design grid's first column, the field name CustomerNum appears in the Field text box, the table name Customer appears in the Table text box, and the check mark in the Show check box indicates that the field will be displayed in the datasheet when you run the query. Sometimes you might not want to display a field and its values in the query results. For example, if you are creating a query to show all customers located in Michigan, and you assign the name "Customers in Michigan" to the query, you do not need to include the State field value for each record in the query results—every State field value would be "MI" for Michigan. Even if you choose not to include a field in the display of the query results, you can still use the field as part of the query to select specific records or to specify a particular sequence for the records in the datasheet.

2. Double-click **CustomerName** in the Customer field list. Access adds this field to the second column of the design grid.

3. Scrolling the Customer field list as necessary, repeat Step 2 for the **City**, **OwnerName**, and **FirstContact** fields to add these fields to the design grid in that order.

Having selected the fields for Kim's query, you can now run the query.

TROUBLE? If you double-click the wrong field and accidentally add it to the design grid, you can remove the field from the grid. Select the field's column by clicking the pointer ↓ on the bar above the Field text box for the field you want to delete, click Edit on the menu bar, and then click Delete Columns.

4. Click the **Run** button on the Query Design toolbar. Access runs the query and displays the results in Datasheet view. See Figure 3-4.

Figure 3-4	DATASHEET DISPLAYED AFTER RUNNING THE QUERY

selected fields displayed

38 records selected

CustomerNum	CustomerName	City	OwnerName	FirstContact
104	Meadows Restaurant	Monroe	Mr. Ray Suchecki	02/28/1991
107	Cottage Grill	Bootjack	Ms. Doris Reaume	04/03/1991
122	Roadhouse Restaurant	Clare	Ms. Shirley Woodruff	04/12/1991
123	Bridge Inn	Ada	Mr. Wayne Bouwman	04/17/1992
128	Grand River Restaurant	Lacota	Mr. John Rohrs	04/20/1992
129	Sandy Lookout Restaurant	Jenison	Ms. Michele Yasenak	04/27/1992
131	Bunker Hill Grill	Eagle Point	Mr. Ronald Kooienga	05/01/1992
133	Florentine Restaurante	Drenthe	Mr. Donald Bench	05/03/1993
135	Topview Restaurant	Zeeland	Ms. Janice Stapleton	05/11/1993
136	Cleo's Downtown Restaurant	Borculo	Ms. Joan Hoffman	05/11/1993
163	Bentham's Riverfront Restaurant	Roscommon	Mr. Joe Markovicz	05/18/1994
165	Sullivan's Restaurant & Lounge	Saugatuck	Ms. Dawn Parker	05/19/1994
201	Wagon Train Restaurant	Selkirk	Mr. Carl Seaver	05/25/1994
202	Extra Helpings Restaurant	Five Lakes	Ms. Deborah Wolfe	05/25/1995
203	Mountain Lake Restaurant	Grand Rapids	Mr. Donald MacPherson	08/25/1995
322	Alto Country Inn	Alto	Mr. James Cowan	06/02/1996
325	Best Bet Restaurant	Grand Rapids	Ms. Rebecca Van Singel	06/12/1996
407	Jean's Country Restaurant	Mattawan	Ms. Jean Brooks	09/18/1996
423	Bay Pointe Restaurant	Shelbyville	Mr. Janosfi Petofi	10/24/1996
515	Cheshire Restaurant	Burlington	Mr. Jeffrey Hersha	12/11/1996
597	Around the Clock Restaurant	Copper Harbor	Ms. Jennifer Lewis	06/24/1997
620	Brandywine Restaurant	Kearsarge	Mr. Walter Reed	07/02/1997
624	South Bend Brewing Company	South Bend	Mr. Toby Stein	07/17/1997
625	Maxwell's Restaurant	South Bend	Ms. Barbara Feldon	07/19/1997
627	Monarch Restaurant	Toledo	Mr. Gilbert Scholten	07/29/1997
635	Oaks Restaurant	Maumee	Ms. Julie Pfeiffer	09/13/1998
646	Golden Gate Restaurant	Romulus	Ms. Nancy Mills	11/12/1998
650	The Peppermill	Elkhart	Ms. Tara Jerentowski	11/16/1998

Record: 1 of 38

The five fields you added to the design grid appear in the datasheet, and the records are displayed in primary key sequence by customer number. Access selected a total of 38 records for display in the datasheet.

Kim asks you to save the query as "Customer Analysis" so that she can easily retrieve the same data again.

5. Click the **Save** button on the Query Datasheet toolbar. The Save As dialog box opens.

6. Type **Customer Analysis** in the Query Name text box, and then press the **Enter** key. Access saves the query with the specified name in the Restaurant database on your Data Disk and displays the name in the title bar.

7. Click the **Close** button on the menu bar to close the query and return to the Database window. Note that the Customer Analysis query appears in the list of queries.

8. Click the **Restore** button on the menu bar to return the Database window to its original size.

Barbara also wants to view specific information in the Restaurant database. However, she needs to see data from both the Customer table and the Order table at the same time. To view data from two tables at the same time, you need to define a relationship between the tables.

Defining **Table Relationships**

One of the most powerful features of a relational database management system is its ability to define relationships between tables. You use a common field to relate one table to another. The process of relating tables is often called performing a **join**. When you join tables that have a common field, you can extract data from them as if they were one larger table. For example, you can join the Customer and Order tables by using the CustomerNum field in both tables as the common field. Then you can use a query, form, or report to extract selected data from each table, even though the data is contained in two separate tables, as shown in Figure 3-5. In the Orders query shown in Figure 3-5, the OrderNum, Paid, and InvoiceAmt columns are fields from the Order table, and the CustomerName and State columns are fields from the Customer table. The joining of records is based on the common field of CustomerNum. The Customer and Order tables have a type of relationship called a one-to-many relationship.

Figure 3-5	ONE-TO-MANY RELATIONSHIP AND SAMPLE QUERY

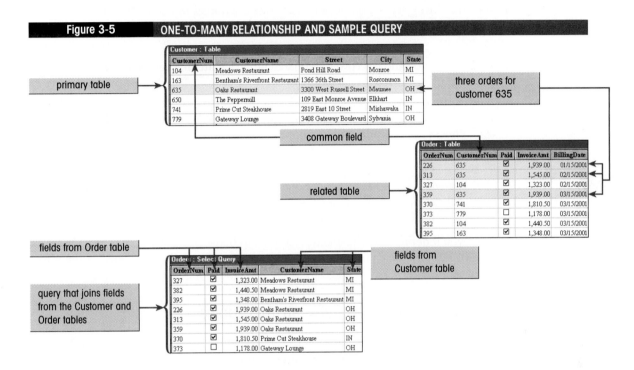

One-to-Many Relationships

A **one-to-many relationship** exists between two tables when one record in the first table matches zero, one, or many records in the second table, and when one record in the second table matches exactly one record in the first table. For example, as shown in Figure 3-5, customer 635 has three orders, customer 650 has zero orders, customers 163, 741, and 779 each have one order, and customer 104 has two orders. Every order has a single matching customer.

Access refers to the two tables that form a relationship as the primary table and the related table. The **primary table** is the "one" table in a one-to-many relationship; in Figure 3-5, the Customer table is the primary table because there is only one customer for each order. The **related table** is the "many" table; in Figure 3-5, the Order table is the related table because there can be many orders for each customer.

Because related data is stored in two tables, inconsistencies between the tables can occur. Consider the following scenarios:

- Barbara adds an order to the Order table for customer 107, Cottage Grill. This order does not have a matching record in the Customer table. The data is inconsistent, and the order record is considered to be an **orphaned** record.

- Barbara changes Oaks Restaurant from customer number 635 to 997 in the Customer table. Three orphaned records for customer 635 now exist in the Order table, and the database is inconsistent.

■ Barbara deletes the record for Meadows Restaurant, customer 104, in the Customer table because this customer is no longer a Valle Coffee customer. The database is again inconsistent; two records for customer 104 in the Order table have no matching record in the Customer table.

You can avoid these problems by specifying referential integrity between tables when you define their relationships.

Referential Integrity

Referential integrity is a set of rules that Access enforces to maintain consistency between related tables when you update data in a database. Specifically, the referential integrity rules are as follows:

■ When you add a record to a related table, a matching record must already exist in the primary table.

■ If you attempt to change the value of the primary key in the primary table, Access prevents this change if matching records exist in a related table. However, if you choose the **cascade updates** option, Access permits the change in value to the primary key and changes the appropriate foreign key values in the related table.

■ When you delete a record in the primary table, Access prevents the deletion if matching records exist in a related table. However, if you choose the **cascade deletes** option, Access deletes the record in the primary table and all records in related tables that have matching foreign key values.

Now you'll define a one-to-many relationship between the Customer and Order tables so that you can use fields from both tables to create a query that will retrieve the information Barbara wants.

Defining a Relationship Between Two Tables

When two tables have a common field, you can define a relationship between them in the Relationships window. The **Relationships window** illustrates the relationships among a database's tables. In this window you can view or change existing relationships, define new relationships between tables, and rearrange the layout of the tables.

You need to open the Relationships window and define the relationship between the Customer and Order tables. You'll define a one-to-many relationship between the two tables, with Customer as the primary table and Order as the related table, and with CustomerNum as the common field (the primary key in the Customer table and a foreign key in the Order table).

To define a one-to-many relationship between the two tables:

1. Click the **Relationships** button [icon] on the Database toolbar. The Show Table dialog box opens on top of the Relationships window. See Figure 3-6.

Figure 3-6	SHOW TABLE DIALOG BOX

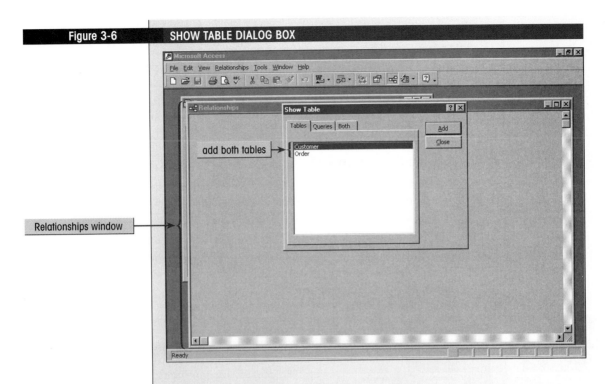

You must add each table participating in a relationship to the Relationships window.

2. Click **Customer** (if necessary) and then click the **Add** button. The Customer table is added to the Relationships window.

3. Click **Order** and then click the **Add** button. The Order table is added to the Relationships window.

4. Click the **Close** button in the Show Table dialog box to close it and reveal the entire Relationships window.

To form the relationship between the two tables, you drag the common field of CustomerNum from the primary table to the related table. Then Access opens the Edit Relationships dialog box, in which you select the relationship options for the two tables.

5. Click **CustomerNum** in the Customer table list, and drag it to **CustomerNum** in the Order table list. When you release the mouse button, the Edit Relationships dialog box opens. See Figure 3-7.

Figure 3-7	EDIT RELATIONSHIPS DIALOG BOX

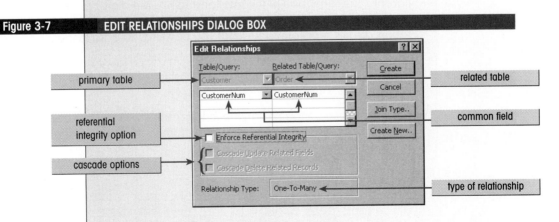

The primary table, related table, and common field appear at the top of the dialog box. The type of relationship, one-to-many, appears at the bottom of the dialog box. When you click the Enforce Referential Integrity check box, the two cascade options become available. If you select the Cascade Update Related Fields option, Access will change the appropriate foreign key values in the related table when you change a primary key value in the primary table. If you select the Cascade Delete Related Records option, when you delete a record in the primary table, Access will delete all records in the related table that have a matching foreign key value.

6. Click the **Enforce Referential Integrity** check box, click the **Cascade Update Related Fields** check box, and then click the **Cascade Delete Related Records** check box. You have now selected all the necessary relationship options.

7. Click the **Create** button to define the one-to-many relationship between the two tables and close the dialog box. The completed relationship appears in the Relationships window. See Figure 3-8.

Figure 3-8	DEFINED RELATIONSHIP IN THE RELATIONSHIPS WINDOW

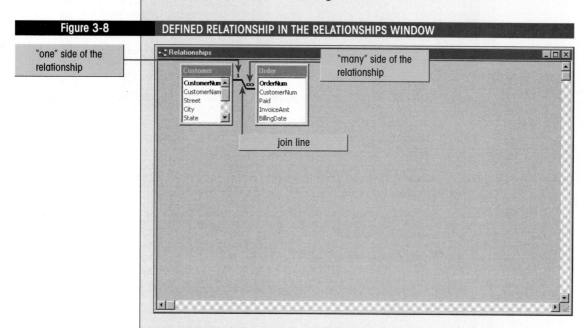

"one" side of the relationship

"many" side of the relationship

join line

The **join line** connects the CustomerNum fields, which are common to the two tables. The common field joins the two tables, which have a one-to-many relationship. The "one" side of the relationship has the digit 1 at its end, and the "many" side of the relationship has the infinity symbol ∞ at its end. The two tables are still separate tables, but you can use the data in them as if they were one table.

8. Click the **Save** button 🖫 on the Relationship toolbar to save the layout in the Relationships window.

9. Click the **Close** button ✕ on the Relationships window title bar. The Relationships window closes, and you return to the Database window.

Now that you have joined the Customer and Order tables, you can create a query to produce the information Barbara wants. As part of her system for tracking payments received from restaurant customers, Barbara needs a query that displays the CustomerName, City, and State fields from the Customer table and the BillingDate, InvoiceAmt, and Paid fields from the Order table.

To create, run, and save the query using the Customer and Order tables:

1. With the Queries object selected in the Database window, double-click **Create query in Design view**. The Show Table dialog box opens on top of the Query window in Design view.

   You need to add both tables to the Query window.

2. Click **Customer** in the Tables list box (if necessary), click the **Add** button, click **Order**, click the **Add** button, and then click the **Close** button. The Customer and Order field lists appear in the Query window, and the Show Table dialog box closes. Note that the one-to-many relationship that exists between the two tables is shown in the Query window. Also, notice that the join line is thick at both ends; this signifies that you selected the option to enforce referential integrity. If you had not selected this option, the join line would be thin at both ends and neither the "1" nor the infinity symbol would appear, even though there is a one-to-many relationship between the two tables.

   You need to place the CustomerName, City, and State fields from the Customer field list into the design grid, and then place the BillingDate, InvoiceAmt, and Paid fields from the Order field list into the design grid.

3. Double-click **CustomerName** in the Customer field list to place CustomerName in the design grid's first column Field text box.

4. Repeat Step 3 to add the **City** and **State** fields from the Customer table, and then add the **BillingDate**, **InvoiceAmt**, and **Paid** fields (in that order) from the Order table, so that these fields are placed in the second through sixth columns of the design grid.

   The query specifications are complete, so you can now run the query.

5. Click the **Run** button ! on the Query Design toolbar. Access runs the query and displays the results in the datasheet.

6. Click the **Maximize** button ▢ on the Query window. See Figure 3-9.

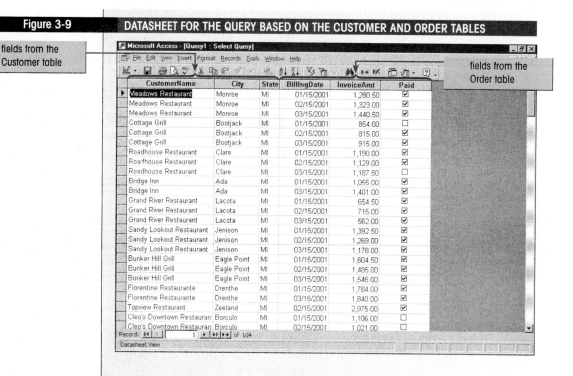

Figure 3-9   **DATASHEET FOR THE QUERY BASED ON THE CUSTOMER AND ORDER TABLES**

fields from the Customer table

fields from the Order table

Only the six selected fields from the Customer and Order tables appear in the datasheet. The records are displayed in order according to the values in the primary key field, CustomerNum, even though this field is not included in the query datasheet.

Barbara plans on frequently tracking the data retrieved by the query, so she asks you to save the query as "Customer Orders."

7. Click the **Save** button 🖫 on the Query Datasheet toolbar. The Save As dialog box opens.

8. Type **Customer Orders** in the Query Name text box, and then press the **Enter** key. Access saves the query with the specified name and displays the name in the Query window title bar.

Barbara decides she wants the records displayed in alphabetical order by customer name. Because your query displays data in order by the field value of CustomerNum, the primary key for the Customer table, you need to sort the records by CustomerName to display the data in the order Barbara wants.

Sorting Data in a Query

Sorting is the process of rearranging records in a specified order or sequence. Often you need to sort data before displaying or printing it, to meet a specific request. For example, Barbara might want to review order information arranged by the Paid field because she needs to know which orders are still unpaid. On the other hand, Leonard might want to view order information arranged by the InvoiceAmt totals for each customer, because he tracks company sales.

When you sort data in a database, you do not change the sequence of the records in the underlying tables. Only the records in the query datasheet are rearranged according to your specifications.

To sort records, you must select the **sort key**, which is the field used to determine the order of records in the datasheet. In this case, Barbara wants the data sorted by the customer name, so you need to specify the CustomerName field as the sort key. Sort keys can be text, number, date/time, currency, AutoNumber, yes/no, or Lookup Wizard fields, but not memo, OLE object, or hyperlink fields. You sort records in either ascending (increasing) or descending (decreasing) order. Figure 3-10 shows the results of each type of sort for different data types.

Figure 3-10	SORTING RESULTS FOR DIFFERENT DATA TYPES	
DATA TYPE	**ASCENDING SORT RESULTS**	**DESCENDING SORT RESULTS**
Text	A to Z	Z to A
Number	lowest to highest numeric value	highest to lowest numeric value
Date/Time	oldest to most recent date	most recent to oldest date
Currency	lowest to highest numeric value	highest to lowest numeric value
AutoNumber	lowest to highest numeric value	highest to lowest numeric value
Yes/No	yes (check mark in check box) then no values	no then yes values

Access provides several methods for sorting data in a table or query datasheet and in a form. One method, clicking the toolbar sort buttons, lets you sort the displayed records quickly.

Using a Toolbar Button to Sort Data

The **Sort Ascending** and **Sort Descending** buttons on the toolbar allow you to sort records immediately, based on the selected field. First you select the column on which you want to base the sort, and then you click the appropriate sort button on the toolbar to rearrange the records in either ascending or descending order. Unless you save the datasheet or form after you've sorted the records, the rearrangement of records is temporary.

Recall that in Tutorial 1 you used the Sort Ascending button to sort query results by the State field. You'll use this same button to sort the Customer Orders query results by the CustomerName field.

To sort the records using a toolbar sort button:

1. Click any visible CustomerName field value to establish this field as the current field.

2. Click the **Sort Ascending** button [icon] on the Query Datasheet toolbar. The records are rearranged in ascending order by customer name. See Figure 3-11.

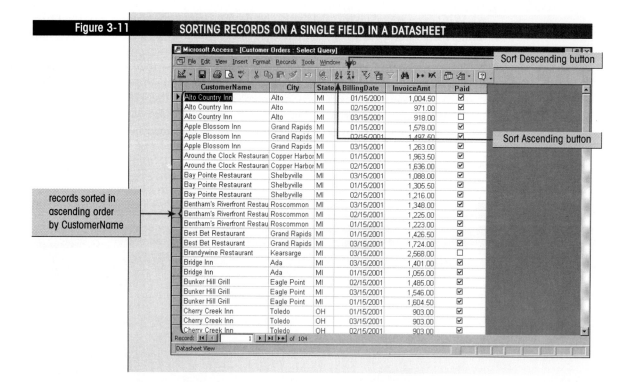

Figure 3-11 — SORTING RECORDS ON A SINGLE FIELD IN A DATASHEET

After viewing the query results, Barbara decides that she'd prefer to see the records arranged by the value in the Paid field, so that she can identify the paid invoices more easily. She wants to view all the unpaid invoices before the paid invoices (descending order for the Paid field, which is a yes/no field); plus, she wants to display the records within each group in increasing value of the InvoiceAmt field. To do this you need to sort using two fields.

Sorting Multiple Fields in Design View

Sort keys can be unique or nonunique. A sort key is **unique** if the value of the sort key field for each record is different. The CustomerNum field in the Customer table is an example of a unique sort key because each customer record has a different value in this field. A sort key is **nonunique** if more than one record can have the same value for the sort key field. For example, the Paid field in the Order table is a nonunique sort key because more than one record has the same Paid value.

When the sort key is nonunique, records with the same sort key value are grouped together, but they are not in a specific order within the group. To arrange these grouped records in a specific order, you can specify a **secondary sort key**, which is a second sort key field. The first sort key field is called the **primary sort key**. Note that the primary sort key is not the same as a table's primary key field. A table has at most one primary key, which must be unique, whereas any field in a table can serve as a primary sort key.

Access lets you select up to 10 different sort keys. When you use the toolbar sort buttons, the sort key fields must be in adjacent columns in the datasheet. You highlight the columns, and Access sorts first by the first column and then by each other highlighted column in order from left to right.

Barbara wants the records sorted first by the Paid field and then by the InvoiceAmt field. Although the two fields are adjacent, they are in the wrong order in your current query design. If you used a toolbar sort button, the InvoiceAmt field would be the primary sort key instead of the Paid field. You could move the InvoiceAmt field to the right of the Paid field in the query datasheet. However, you can specify only one type of sort—either ascending or descending—for selected columns in the query datasheet. This is not what Barbara wants; she wants the Paid field values to be sorted in descending order and the InvoiceAmt field values to be sorted in ascending order.

In this case, you need to specify the sort keys for the query in Design view. Any time you want to sort on multiple fields that are nonadjacent or in the wrong order, but you do not want to rearrange the columns in the query datasheet to accomplish the sort, you must specify the sort keys in Design view.

In the Query window in Design view, Access first uses the sort key that is leftmost in the design grid. Therefore, you must arrange the fields you want to sort from left to right in the design grid, with the primary sort key being the leftmost sort key field.

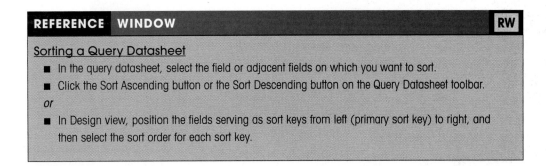

REFERENCE WINDOW   **RW**

Sorting a Query Datasheet
- In the query datasheet, select the field or adjacent fields on which you want to sort.
- Click the Sort Ascending button or the Sort Descending button on the Query Datasheet toolbar.
or
- In Design view, position the fields serving as sort keys from left (primary sort key) to right, and then select the sort order for each sort key.

To achieve the results Barbara wants, you need to switch to Design view, move the InvoiceAmt field to the right of the Paid field, and then specify the sort order for the two fields.

To select the two sort keys in Design view:

1. Click the **View** button for Design view 📐 on the Query Datasheet toolbar to open the query in Design view.

   First, you'll move the InvoiceAmt field to the right of the Paid field.

2. If necessary, click the right arrow in the design grid's horizontal scroll bar a few times to scroll to the right so that both the InvoiceAmt and Paid fields, as well as the next empty column, are completely visible.

3. Position the pointer above the InvoiceAmt field name until the pointer changes to ↓, and then click to select the field. See Figure 3-12.

Figure 3-12	SELECTED INVOICEAMT FIELD

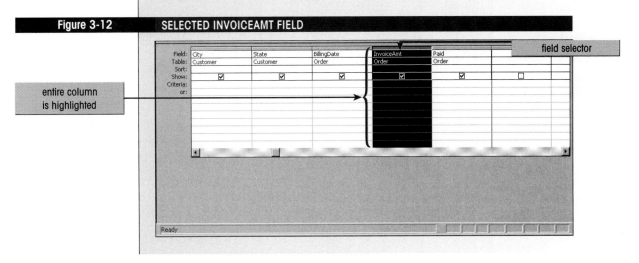

4. Position the pointer in the field selector at the top of the highlighted column, and then click and drag the pointer to the right until the vertical line on the right of the Paid field is highlighted. See Figure 3-13.

Figure 3-13   **DRAGGING THE FIELD IN THE DESIGN GRID**

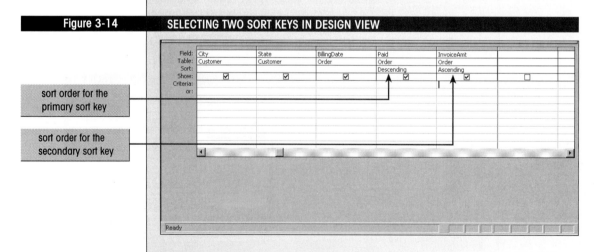

drag pointer to here

line is highlighted

5. Release the mouse button. The InvoiceAmt field moves to the right of the Paid field.

The fields are now in the correct order for the sort. Next, you need to specify a descending sort order for the Paid field and an ascending sort order for the InvoiceAmt field.

6. Click the **Paid Sort** text box, click the **Sort** list arrow that appears, and then click **Descending**. You've selected a descending sort order for the Paid field, which will be the primary sort key. The Paid field is a yes/no field, and a descending sort order for this type of field displays all the no (unpaid) values before the yes (paid) values.

7. Click the **InvoiceAmt Sort** text box, click the **Sort** list arrow, click **Ascending**, and then click the **Criteria** text box for the InvoiceAmt field. You've selected an ascending sort order for the InvoiceAmt field, which will be the secondary sort key. See Figure 3-14.

Figure 3-14   **SELECTING TWO SORT KEYS IN DESIGN VIEW**

sort order for the primary sort key

sort order for the secondary sort key

Field:	City	State	BillingDate	Paid	InvoiceAmt	
Table:	Customer	Customer	Order	Order	Order	
Sort:				Descending	Ascending	
Show:	☑	☑	☑	☑	☑	☐
Criteria:						
or:						

Ready

You have finished your query changes, so now you can run the query and then save the modified query with the same query name.

8. Click the **Run** button ▣ on the Query Design toolbar. Access runs the query and displays the query datasheet. The records appear in descending order, based on the values of the Paid field. Within groups of records with the same Paid field value, the records appear in ascending order by the values of the InvoiceAmt field. See Figure 3-15.

Figure 3-15   **DATASHEET SORTED ON TWO FIELDS**

primary sort key   secondary sort key

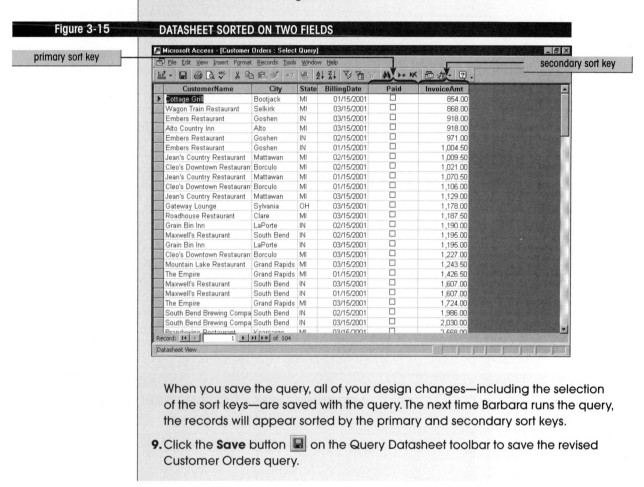

When you save the query, all of your design changes—including the selection of the sort keys—are saved with the query. The next time Barbara runs the query, the records will appear sorted by the primary and secondary sort keys.

9. Click the **Save** button ▣ on the Query Datasheet toolbar to save the revised Customer Orders query.

Barbara wants to concentrate on the unpaid orders in the datasheet. Selecting only the unpaid orders is a temporary change that Barbara wants in the datasheet, so you do not need to switch to Design view and change the query. Instead, you can apply a filter.

Filtering Data

A **filter** is a set of restrictions you place on the records in an open datasheet or form to *temporarily* isolate a subset of the records. A filter lets you view different subsets of displayed records so that you can focus on only the data you need. Unless you save a query or form with a filter applied, an applied filter is not available the next time you run the query or open the form. The simplest technique for filtering records is Filter By Selection. **Filter By Selection** lets you select all or part of a field value in a datasheet or form, and then display only those records that contain the selected value in the field. Another technique for filtering records is to use **Filter By Form**, which changes your datasheet to display empty fields. Then you can select a value from the list arrow that appears when you click any blank field to apply a filter that selects only those records containing that value.

REFERENCE WINDOW   **RW**

<u>Using Filter By Selection</u>
- In the datasheet or form, select all or part of the field value that will be the basis for the filter.
- Click the Filter By Selection button on the toolbar.

For Barbara's request, you need to select an unchecked box in the Paid field, which represents an unpaid order, and then use Filter By Selection to display only those query records with this same value.

To display the records using Filter By Selection:

1. Click any check box that is unchecked in the Paid column. When you click the check box, you select the field value, but you also change the check box from unchecked to checked. Because you've changed an unpaid order to a paid order, you need to click the same check box a second time.

2. Click the same check box a second time. The field value changes back to unchecked, which is now the selected field value.

3. Click the **Filter By Selection** button 🔽 on the Query Datasheet toolbar. Access displays the filtered results. Only the 25 query records that have an unchecked Paid field value appear in the datasheet; these records are the unpaid order records. Note that the status bar display (FLTR), the area next to the navigation buttons, and the selected Remove Filter button on the toolbar all indicate that the records have been filtered. See Figure 3-16.

Figure 3-16	USING FILTER BY SELECTION

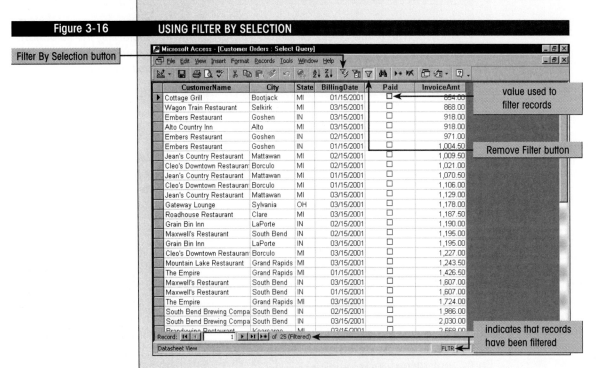

Barbara asks you to print the current datasheet so that she can give the printout to a staff member who is tracking unpaid orders.

4. Click the **Print** button 🖨 on the Query Datasheet toolbar to print the datasheet.

   Now you can redisplay all the query records by clicking the Remove Filter button; this button works as a toggle to switch between the filtered and nonfiltered displays.

5. Click the **Remove Filter** button 🝖 on the Query Datasheet toolbar. Access redisplays all the records in the query datasheet.

6. Click the **Save** button 💾 on the Query Datasheet toolbar, and then click the **Close** button ✖ on the menu bar to save and close the query and return to the Database window.

7. Click the **Restore** button 🗗 on the menu bar to return the Database window to its original size.

The queries you've created will help Valle Coffee employees retrieve just the information they want to view. In the next session, you'll continue to create queries to meet their information needs.

Session 3.1 QUICK CHECK

1. What is a select query?

2. Describe the field list and the design grid in the Query window in Design view.

3. How are a table datasheet and a query datasheet similar? How are they different?

4. The _____ is the "one" table in a one-to-many relationship, and the _____ is the "many" table in the relationship.

5. _____ is a set of rules that Access enforces to maintain consistency between related tables when you update data in a database.

6. For a date/time field, what is ascending sort order?

7. When must you define multiple sort keys in Design view instead of in the query datasheet?

8. A(n) _____ is a set of restrictions you place on the records in an open datasheet or form to isolate a subset of records temporarily.

SESSION 3.2

In this session, you will specify an exact match condition in a query, change a datasheet's appearance, use a comparison operator to match a range of values, use the And and Or logical operators to define multiple selection criteria for queries, and perform calculations in queries.

Barbara wants to display customer and order information for all orders billed on 01/15/2001, so that she can see which orders have been paid. For this request, you need to create a query that displays selected fields from the Order and Customer tables and selected records that satisfy a condition.

Defining **Record Selection Criteria for Queries**

Just as you can display selected fields from a table in a query datasheet, you can display selected records. To tell Access which records you want to select, you must specify a condition as part of the query. A **condition** is a criterion, or rule, that determines which records are selected. To define a condition for a field, you place the condition in the field's Criteria text box in the design grid.

A condition usually consists of an operator, often a comparison operator, and a value. A **comparison operator** asks Access to compare the values of a database field to the condition value and to select all the records for which the relationship is true. For example, the condition >1000.00 for the InvoiceAmt field selects all records in the Order table having InvoiceAmt field values greater than 1000.00. Figure 3-17 shows the Access comparison operators.

Figure 3-17   ACCESS COMPARISON OPERATORS

OPERATOR	MEANING	EXAMPLE
=	equal to (optional; default operator)	="Hall"
<	less than	<#1/1/99#
<=	less than or equal to	<=100
>	greater than	>"C400"
>=	greater than or equal to	>=18.75
<>	not equal to	<>"Hall"
Between ... And...	between two values (inclusive)	Between 50 And 325
In ()	in a list of values	In ("Hall", "Seeger")
Like	matches a pattern that includes wildcards	Like "706*"

Specifying an Exact Match

For Barbara's request, you need to create a query that will display only those records in the Order table with the value 01/15/2001 in the BillingDate field. This type of condition is called an **exact match** because the value in the specified field must match the condition exactly in order for the record to be included in the query results. You'll use the Simple Query Wizard to create the query, and then you'll specify the exact match condition.

To create the query using the Simple Query Wizard:

1. If you took a break after the previous session, make sure that Access is running, the Restaurant database is open, and the Queries object is selected in the Database window.

2. Double-click **Create query by using wizard**. Access opens the first Simple Query Wizard dialog box, in which you select the tables (or queries) and fields for the query.

3. Click the **Tables/Queries** list arrow, and then click **Table: Order**. The fields in the Order table appear in the Available Fields list box. See Figure 3-18.

Figure 3-18	FIRST SIMPLE QUERY WIZARD DIALOG BOX

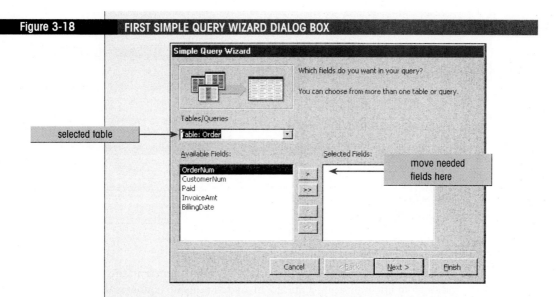

selected table

move needed
fields here

Except for the CustomerNum field, you will include all fields from the Order table in the query.

4. Click the >> button. All the fields from the Available Fields list box move to the Selected Fields list box.

5. Click **CustomerNum** in the Selected Fields list box, click the < button to move the CustomerNum field back to the Available Fields list box, and then click **BillingDate** in the Selected Fields list box.

Barbara also wants certain information from the Customer table included in the query results.

6. Click the **Tables/Queries** list arrow, and then click **Table: Customer**. The fields in the Customer table now appear in the Available Fields list box. Notice that the fields you selected from the Order table remain in the Selected Fields list box.

7. Click **CustomerName** in the Available Fields list box, and then click the > button to move CustomerName to the Selected Fields list box.

8. Repeat Step 7 to move the **State**, **OwnerName**, and **Phone** fields into the Selected Fields list box.

9. Click the **Next** button to open the second Simple Query Wizard dialog box, in which you choose whether the query will display records from the selected tables or a summary of those records. Summary options show calculations such as average, minimum, maximum, and so on. Barbara wants to view the details for the records, not a summary.

10. Make sure the **Detail (shows every field of every record)** option button is selected, and then click the **Next** button to open the last Simple Query Wizard dialog box, in which you choose a name for the query and complete the Wizard. You need to enter a condition for the query, so you'll want to modify the query's design.

11. Type **January Orders**, click the **Modify the query design** option button, and then click the **Finish** button. Access saves the query as January Orders and opens the query in Design view. See Figure 3-19.

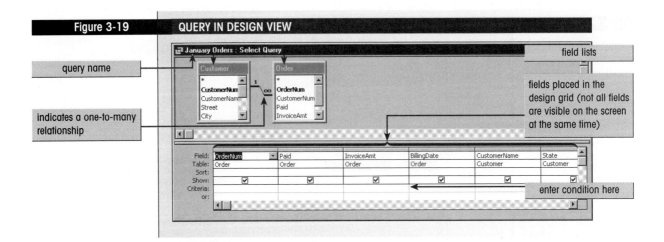

Figure 3-19   QUERY IN DESIGN VIEW

The field lists for the Customer and Order tables appear in the top portion of the window, and the join line indicating a one-to-many relationship connects the two tables. The selected fields appear in the design grid. Not all of the fields are visible in the grid; to see the other selected fields, you need to scroll to the right using the horizontal scroll bar.

To display the information Barbara wants, you need to enter the condition for the BillingDate field in its Criteria text box. Barbara wants to display only those records with a billing date of 01/15/2001.

To enter the exact match condition, and then run the query:

1. Click the **BillingDate Criteria** text box, type **1/15/01**, and then press the **Enter** key. The condition changes to #1/15/01#. (Note that you do not have to type the date as 01/15/2001; if you did, Access would still change the condition to #1/15/01#.)

   Access automatically placed number signs (#) before and after the condition. You must place date and time values inside number signs when using these values as selection criteria. If you omit the number signs, however, Access will include them automatically.

2. Click the **Run** button ![run] on the Query Design toolbar. Access runs the query and displays the selected field values for only those records with a BillingDate field value of 01/15/2001. A total of 36 records are selected and displayed in the datasheet. See Figure 3-20.

Figure 3-20   DATASHEET DISPLAYING SELECTED FIELDS AND RECORDS

Barbara would like to see more fields and records on the screen at one time. She asks you to maximize the datasheet, change the datasheet's font size, and resize all the columns to their best fit.

Changing a Datasheet's Appearance

You can change the characteristics of a datasheet, including the font type and size of text in the datasheet, to improve its appearance or readability. You also can resize the datasheet columns to view more columns on the screen at the same time.

You'll maximize the datasheet, change the font size from the default 10 points to 8, and then resize the datasheet columns.

To change the font size and resize columns in the datasheet:

1. Click the **Maximize** button 🗖 on the Query window title bar.

2. Click the **record selector** to the left of the field names at the top of the datasheet (see Figure 3-20) to select the entire datasheet.

3. Click **Format** on the menu bar, and then click **Font** to open the Font dialog box.

4. Scroll the Size list box, click **8**, and then click the **OK** button. The font size for the entire datasheet changes to 8.

   Next you need to resize the columns to their best fit—that is, so each column is just wide enough to fit the longest value in the column.

5. Position the pointer in the OrderNum field selector. When the pointer changes to ↓, click to select the entire column and deselect all other columns.

6. Click the horizontal scroll right arrow until the Phone field is fully visible, and then position the pointer in the Phone field selector until the pointer changes to ↓.

7. Press and hold the **Shift** key, and then click the mouse button. All the columns are selected. Now you can resize all of them at once.

8. Position the pointer at the right edge of the Phone field selector until the pointer changes to ↔. See Figure 3-21.

| Figure 3-21 | PREPARING TO RESIZE ALL COLUMNS TO THEIR BEST FIT |

all columns selected

column resizing pointer

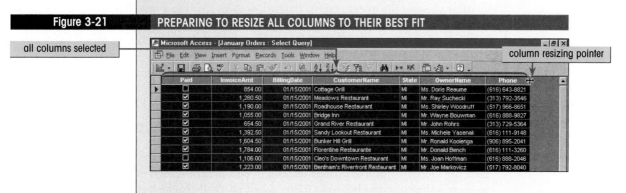

9. Double-click the mouse button. All columns are resized to their best fit, which makes each column just large enough to fit the longest *visible* field value in the column, including the field name at the top of the column. Scroll through the datasheet and resize individual columns as needed to display all field values completely.

10. If necessary, scroll to the left so that the OrderNum field is visible, and then click any field value box (except a Paid field value) to deselect all columns. See Figure 3-22.

| Figure 3-22 | DATASHEET AFTER CHANGING FONT SIZE AND COLUMN WIDTHS |

OrderNum	Paid	InvoiceAmt	BillingDate	CustomerName	State	OwnerName	Phone
201	☐	854.00	01/15/2001	Cottage Grill	MI	Ms. Doris Reaume	(616) 643-8821
202	☑	1,280.50	01/15/2001	Meadows Restaurant	MI	Mr. Ray Suchecki	(313) 792-3546
203	☑	1,190.00	01/15/2001	Roadhouse Restaurant	MI	Ms. Shirley Woodruff	(517) 966-8651
204	☑	1,055.00	01/15/2001	Bridge Inn	MI	Mr. Wayne Bouwman	(616) 888-9827
205	☑	654.50	01/15/2001	Grand River Restaurant	MI	Mr. John Rohrs	(313) 729-5364
206	☑	1,392.50	01/15/2001	Sandy Lookout Restaurant	MI	Ms. Michele Yasenak	(616) 111-9148
207	☑	1,604.50	01/15/2001	Bunker Hill Grill	MI	Mr. Ronald Kooienga	(906) 895-2041
208	☑	1,784.00	01/15/2001	Florentine Restaurante	MI	Mr. Donald Bench	(616) 111-3260
209	☐	1,106.00	01/15/2001	Cleo's Downtown Restaurant	MI	Ms. Joan Hoffman	(616) 888-2046
210	☑	1,223.00	01/15/2001	Bentham's Riverfront Restaurant	MI	Mr. Joe Markovicz	(517) 792-8040
211	☑	703.50	01/15/2001	Wagon Train Restaurant	MI	Mr. Carl Seaver	(517) 111-5545
212	☑	1,220.50	01/15/2001	Mountain Lake Restaurant	MI	Mr. Donald MacPherson	(616) 532-4499
213	☑	1,426.50	01/15/2001	Best Bet Restaurant	MI	Ms. Rebecca Van Singel	(616) 415-7294
214	☐	1,070.50	01/15/2001	Jean's Country Restaurant	MI	Ms. Jean Brooks	(517) 620-4431
215	☑	1,852.00	01/15/2001	Prime Cut Steakhouse	IN	Ms. Gretchen Fletcher	(219) 336-0900
216	☑	1,309.50	01/15/2001	Cheshire Restaurant	MI	Mr. Jeffrey Hersha	(517) 717-9855
217	☑	1,963.50	01/15/2001	Around the Clock Restaurant	MI	Ms. Jennifer Lewis	(906) 273-9465
218	☑	1,530.00	01/15/2001	Monarch Restaurant	OH	Mr. Gilbert Scholten	(419) 332-2681
219	☑	1,578.00	01/15/2001	Apple Blossom Inn	MI	Ms. Pam Leonard	(616) 755-1736
220	☑	1,248.50	01/15/2001	Extra Helpings Restaurant	MI	Ms. Deborah Wolfe	(517) 889-6003
221	☐	1,607.00	01/15/2001	Maxwell's Restaurant	IN	Ms. Barbara Feldon	(219) 333-0000
222	☑	1,986.00	01/15/2001	South Bend Brewing Company	IN	Mr. Toby Stein	(219) 332-4847
223	☑	1,129.00	01/15/2001	The Brittany Restaurant	MI	Mr. Ken Hodge	(517) 331-7388
224	☑	1,004.50	01/15/2001	Alto Country Inn	MI	Mr. James Cowan	(616) 888-7111
225	☑	2,363.00	01/15/2001	Four Star Steakhouse	MI	Mr. Gregory Olson	(906) 434-4192
226	☑	1,939.00	01/15/2001	Oaks Restaurant	OH	Ms. Julie Pfeiffer	(419) 336-9000
227	☑	1,505.00	01/15/2001	The Peppermill	IN	Ms. Tara Jerentowski	(219) 334-3980
228	☑	903.00	01/15/2001	Cherry Creek Inn	OH	Mr. Douglas Viereck	(419) 336-2333

Record: |◄ ◄| 1 |► ►| |►*| of 36

primary key

TROUBLE? Your screen might show more or fewer rows, depending on the monitor you are using.

11. Click the **Save** button 🖫 on the Query Datasheet toolbar, and then click the **Close** button ☒ on the menu bar. Access saves and closes the query, and you return to the Database window.

After viewing the query results, Barbara decides that she would like to see the same fields, but only for those records whose InvoiceAmt exceeds $2,000. She wants to note this information and pass it along to her staff members so that they can contact those customers with higher outstanding invoices. To create the query needed to produce these results, you need to use a comparison operator to match a range of values—in this case, any InvoiceAmt value greater than $2,000.

Using a Comparison Operator to Match a Range of Values

Once you create and save a query, you can click the Open button to run it again, or you can click the Design button to change its design. Because the design of the query you need to create next is similar to the January Orders query, you will change its design, run the query to test it, and then save the query with a new name, which keeps the January Orders query intact.

To change the January Orders query design to create a new query:

1. Click the **January Orders** query in the Database window (if necessary), and then click the **Design** button to open the January Orders query in Design view.

2. Click the **InvoiceAmt Criteria** text box, type **>2000**, and then press the **Tab** key. See Figure 3-23.

| Figure 3-23 | CHANGING A QUERY'S DESIGN TO CREATE A NEW QUERY |

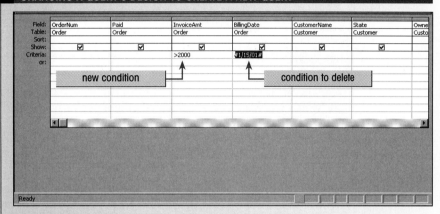

Barbara's new condition specifies that a record will be selected only if its InvoiceAmt field value exceeds 2000. Before you run the query, you need to delete the condition for the BillingDate field.

3. With the BillingDate field condition highlighted, press the **Delete** key. Now there is no condition for the BillingDate field.

4. Click the **Run** button [!] on the Query Design toolbar. Access runs the query and displays the selected fields for only those records with an InvoiceAmt field value greater than 2000. A total of four records are selected. See Figure 3-24.

| Figure 3-24 | RUNNING THE MODIFIED QUERY |

only records with an InvoiceAmt value greater than 2000 are selected

Of the records retrieved, Barbara notes that order numbers 365 and 387 have not yet been paid and the amount of each. She gives this information to her staff.

So that Barbara can display this information again, as necessary, you'll save the query as High Invoice Amounts.

5. Click **File** on the menu bar, and then click **Save As** to open the Save As dialog box.

6. In the text box for the new query name, type **High Invoice Amounts**. Notice that the As text box specifies that you are saving the data as a query.

7. Click the **OK** button to save the query using the new name. The new query name appears in the Query window title bar.

8. Click the **Close** button ☒ on the menu bar. The Database window becomes the active window.

Leonard asks Barbara for a list of the orders billed on 01/15/2001 that are still unpaid. He wants to know which customers are slow in paying their invoices. To produce this data, you need to create a query containing two conditions—one for the order's billing date and another to indicate that the order is unpaid.

Defining **Multiple Selection Criteria for Queries**

Multiple conditions require you to use **logical operators** to combine two or more conditions. When you want a record selected only if two or more conditions are met, you need to use the **And logical operator**. In this case, Leonard wants to see only those records with a BillingDate field value of 01/15/2001 *and* a Paid field value of No. If you place conditions in separate fields in the *same* Criteria row of the design grid, all the conditions in that row must be met in order for a record to be included in the query results. However, if you place conditions in *different* Criteria rows, a record will be selected if at least one of the conditions is met. If none of the conditions is met, then Access does not select the record. When you place conditions in different Criteria rows, you are using the **Or logical operator**. Figure 3-25 illustrates the difference between the And and Or logical operators.

Figure 3-25	LOGICAL OPERATORS And AND Or FOR MULTIPLE SELECTION CRITERIA

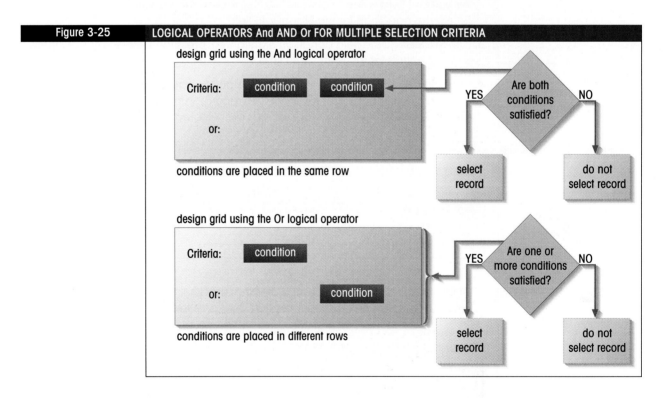

The And Logical Operator

To create Leonard's query, you need to modify the existing January Orders query to show only the unpaid orders billed on 01/15/2001. For the modified query, you must add a second condition in the same Criteria row. The condition #1/15/01# for the BillingDate field finds records billed on the specified date, and the condition "No" in the Paid field finds records whose invoices have not been paid. Because the conditions appear in the same Criteria row, the query will select records only if both conditions are met.

After modifying the query, you'll save it and then rename it as "Unpaid January Orders," overwriting the January Orders query, which Barbara no longer needs.

To modify the January Orders query and use the And logical operator:

1. With the Queries object selected in the Database window, click **January Orders** (if necessary), and then click the **Design** button to open the query in Design view.

2. Click the **Paid Criteria** text box, type **no**, and then press the **Tab** key. See Figure 3-26.

| Figure 3-26 | QUERY TO FIND UNPAID JANUARY ORDERS |

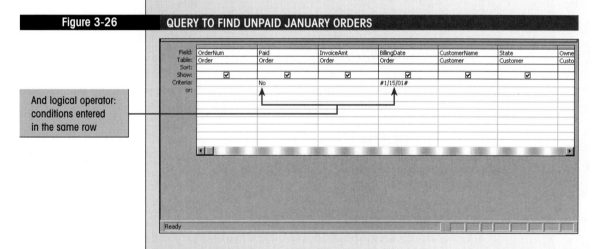

And logical operator: conditions entered in the same row

The condition for the BillingDate field is already entered, so you can run the query.

3. Click the **Run** button on the Query Design toolbar. Access runs the query and displays in the datasheet only those records that meet both conditions: a BillingDate field value of 01/15/2001 and a Paid field value of No. A total of six records are selected. See Figure 3-27.

| Figure 3-27 | RESULTS OF QUERY USING THE AND LOGICAL OPERATOR |

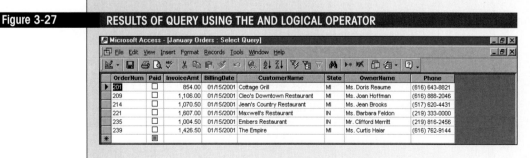

Now you can save the changes to the query and rename it.

4. Click the **Save** button 🔲 on the Query Datasheet toolbar, and then click the **Close** button ⊠ on the menu bar.

5. Right-click **January Orders** in the Queries list box, and then click **Rename** on the shortcut menu.

6. Click to position the insertion point to the left of the word "January," type **Unpaid**, press the **spacebar**, and then press the **Enter** key. The query name is now Unpaid January Orders.

Leonard also wants to determine which restaurant customers are most valuable to Valle Coffee. Specifically, he wants to see a list of those customers who have been placing orders for many years or who place orders for a substantial amount of money, so that he can call the customers personally and thank them for their business. To create this query, you need to use the Or logical operator.

The Or Logical Operator

For Leonard's request, you need a query that selects records when either one of two conditions is satisfied or when both conditions are satisfied. That is, a record is selected if the FirstContact field value is less than 01/1/1994 (to find those customers who have been doing business with Valle Coffee the longest) *or* if the InvoiceAmt field value is greater than 2000 (to find those customers who spend more money). You will enter the condition for the FirstContact field in one Criteria row and the condition for the InvoiceAmt field in another Criteria row, thereby using the Or logical operator.

To display the information Leonard wants to view, you'll create a new query containing the CustomerName, OwnerName, Phone, and FirstContact fields from the Customer table and the InvoiceAmt field from the Order table. Then you'll specify the conditions using the Or logical operator.

To create the query and use the Or logical operator:

1. In the Database window, double-click **Create query in Design view**. The Show Table dialog box opens on top of the Query window in Design view.

2. Click **Customer** in the Tables list box (if necessary), click the **Add** button, click **Order**, click the **Add** button, and then click the **Close** button. The Customer and Order field lists appear in the Query window and the Show Table dialog box closes.

3. Double-click **CustomerName** in the Customer field list to add the CustomerName field to the design grid's first column Field text box.

4. Repeat Step 3 to add the **OwnerName**, **Phone**, and **FirstContact** fields from the Customer table, and then add the **InvoiceAmt** field from the Order table.

   Now you need to specify the first condition, <1/1/94, in the FirstContact field.

5. Click the **FirstContact Criteria** text box, type **<1/1/94** and then press the **Tab** key.

   Because you want records selected if either of the conditions for the FirstContact or InvoiceAmt fields is satisfied, you must enter the condition for the InvoiceAmt field in the "or" row of the design grid.

6. Press the ↓ key, and then type **>2000** in the "or" text box for InvoiceAmt. See Figure 3-28.

Figure 3-28	QUERY WINDOW WITH THE OR LOGICAL OPERATOR

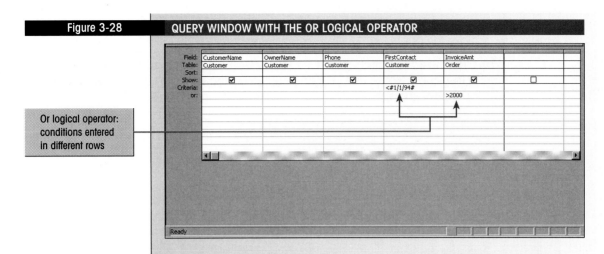

Or logical operator: conditions entered in different rows

The query specifications are complete, so now you can run the query.

7. Click the **Run** button ☝ on the Query Design toolbar. Access runs the query and displays only those records that meet either condition: a FirstContact field value less than 01/1/1994 or an InvoiceAmt field value greater than 2000. A total of 29 records are selected.

Leonard wants the list displayed in alphabetical order by CustomerName.

8. Click any visible CustomerName field value to establish this field as the current field, and then click the **Sort Ascending** button ☝ on the Query Datasheet toolbar.

9. Resize all datasheet columns to their best fit. Be sure to scroll through the entire datasheet to make sure that all values are completely displayed. Deselect all columns when finished resizing, and then return to the top of the datasheet. See Figure 3-29.

Figure 3-29	RESULTS OF QUERY USING THE OR LOGICAL OPERATOR

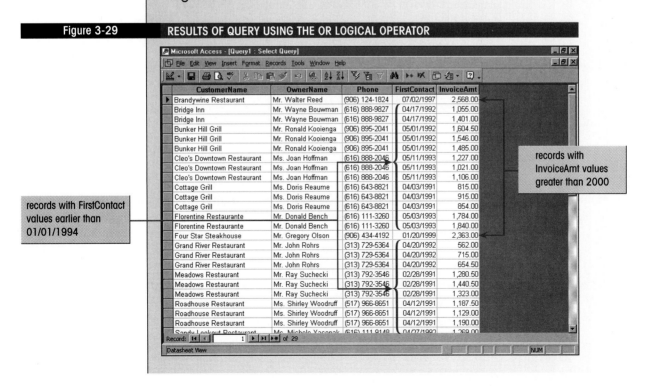

records with FirstContact values earlier than 01/01/1994

records with InvoiceAmt values greater than 2000

> Now you'll save the query as Top Customers, print the query results, and then close the query.
>
> **10.** Click the **Save** button 🖫 on the Query Datasheet toolbar, type **Top Customers** in the Query Name text box, and then press the **Enter** key. Access saves the query with the specified name in the Restaurant database.
>
> **11.** Click the **Print** button 🖨 on the Query Datasheet toolbar to print the query results, and then click the **Close** button ✕ on the menu bar to close the query and return to the Database window.

Next, Leonard asks Barbara if the Restaurant database can be used to perform calculations. He is considering adding a 2% late charge to the unpaid invoices billed in January, and he wants to know exactly what these charges would be.

Performing **Calculations**

In addition to using queries to retrieve, sort, and filter data in a database, you can use a query to perform calculations. To perform a calculation, you define an **expression** containing a combination of database fields, constants, and operators. For numeric expressions, the data types of the database fields must be number, currency, or date/time; the constants are numbers such as .02 (for the 2% late charge); and the operators can be arithmetic operators (+ – * /) or other specialized operators. In complex expressions you can enclose calculations in parentheses to indicate which one should be performed first. In expressions without parentheses, Access calculates in the following order of precedence: multiplication and division before addition and subtraction. When operators have equal precedence, Access calculates them in order from left to right.

To perform a calculation in a query, you add a calculated field to the query. A **calculated field** is a field that displays the results of an expression. A calculated field appears in a query datasheet; however, it does not exist in a database. When you run a query that contains a calculated field, Access evaluates the expression defined by the calculated field and displays the resulting value in the datasheet.

Creating a Calculated Field

To produce the information Leonard wants, you need to open the Unpaid January Orders query and create a calculated field that will multiply each InvoiceAmt field value by .02 to account for the 2% late charge Leonard is considering.

To enter an expression for a calculated field, you can type it directly in a Field text box in the design grid. Alternatively, you can open the Zoom box or Expression Builder and use either one to enter the expression. The **Zoom box** is a large text box for entering text, expressions, or other values. **Expression Builder** is an Access tool that contains an expression box for entering the expression, buttons for common operators, and one or more lists of expression elements, such as table and field names. Unlike a Field text box, which is too small to show an entire expression at one time, the Zoom box and Expression Builder are large enough to display lengthy expressions. In most cases Expression Builder provides the easiest way to enter expressions.

REFERENCE WINDOW	RW

Using Expression Builder
- Display the query in Design view.
- In the design grid, position the insertion point in the Field text box of the field for which you want to create an expression.
- Click the Build button on the Query Design toolbar.
- Use the expression elements and common operators to build the expression, or type the expression directly.
- Click the OK button.

You'll begin by opening the Unpaid January Orders query in Design view and modifying it to show only the information Leonard wants to view.

To modify the Unpaid January Orders query:

1. In the Database window, click **Unpaid January Orders**, and then click the **Design** button.

   Leonard wants to see only the OrderNum, CustomerName, and InvoiceAmt fields. So, you'll first delete the unnecessary fields, and then uncheck the Show boxes for the Paid and BillingDate fields. You need to keep these two fields in the query because they specify the conditions for the query; however, Leonard does not want them to appear in the query results.

2. Scroll the design grid to the right until the last three fields—State, OwnerName, and Phone—are visible.

3. Position the pointer on the State field until the pointer changes to ↓, click and hold down the mouse button, drag the mouse to the right to highlight the State, OwnerName, and Phone fields, and then release the mouse button.

4. Press the **Delete** key to delete the three selected fields.

5. Scroll the design grid back to the left, click the **Show** check box for the Paid field to remove the check mark, and then click the **Show** check box for the BillingDate field to remove the check mark.

   Next you'll move the InvoiceAmt field to the right of the CustomerName field so that the InvoiceAmt values will appear next to the calculated field values in the query results.

6. Make sure both the InvoiceAmt field and the empty field to the right of the CustomerName field are visible in the design grid.

7. Select the InvoiceAmt field, and then use the pointer ⟍ to drag the field to the right of the CustomerName field.

8. If necessary, scroll the design grid so that the empty field to the right of InvoiceAmt is visible, and then click anywhere in the design grid to deselect the InvoiceAmt field. See Figure 3-30.

Figure 3-30   MODIFIED QUERY BEFORE ADDING THE CALCULATED FIELD

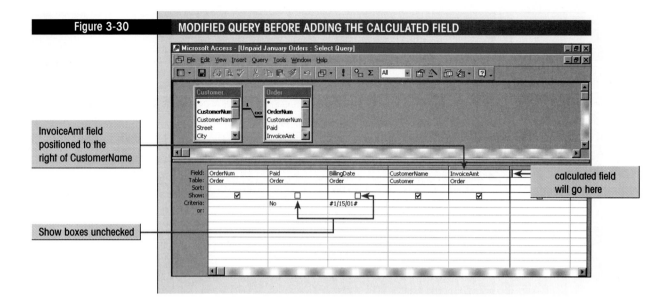

InvoiceAmt field positioned to the right of CustomerName

calculated field will go here

Show boxes unchecked

Now you're ready to use Expression Builder to enter the calculated field in the Unpaid January Orders query.

To add the calculated field to the Unpaid January Orders query:

1. Position the insertion point in the Field text box to the right of the InvoiceAmt field, and then click the **Build** button on the Query Design toolbar. The Expression Builder dialog box opens. See Figure 3-31.

Figure 3-31   INITIAL EXPRESSION BUILDER DIALOG BOX

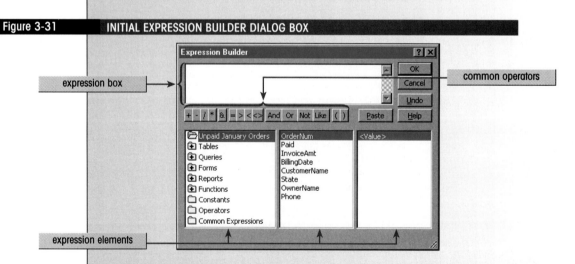

expression box

common operators

expression elements

You use the common operators and expression elements to help you build an expression. Note that the Unpaid January Orders query is already selected in the list box on the lower left; the fields included in the query are listed in the center box.

The expression for the calculated field will multiply the InvoiceAmt field values by the numeric constant .02 (which represents a 2% late charge). To include a field in the expression, you select the field and then click the Paste button. To include a numeric constant, you simply type the constant in the expression.

2. Click **InvoiceAmt** and then click the **Paste** button. [InvoiceAmt] appears in the expression box.

   To include the multiplication operator in the expression, you click the asterisk (*) button.

3. Click the * button in the row of common operators, and then type **.02**. You have completed the entry of the expression. See Figure 3-32.

Figure 3-32	COMPLETED EXPRESSION FOR THE CALCULATED FIELD

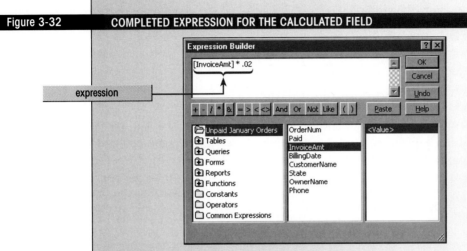

expression

Note that you also could have typed the expression directly into the expression box, instead of clicking the field name and the operator.

4. Click the **OK** button. Access closes the Expression Builder dialog box and adds the expression to the design grid in the Field text box for the calculated field.

   Next, you need to specify a name for the calculated field as it will appear in the query results.

5. Press the **Home** key to position the insertion point to the left of the expression.

   You'll enter the name LateCharge, which is descriptive of the field's contents; then you'll run the query.

6. Type **LateCharge:**. *Make sure you include the colon following the field name.* The colon is needed to separate the field name from its expression.

   Now you can run the query.

7. Click the **Run** button on the Query Design toolbar. Access runs the query and displays the query datasheet, which contains the three specified fields and the calculated field with the name "LateCharge." See Figure 3-33.

Figure 3-33	DATASHEET DISPLAYING THE CALCULATED FIELD

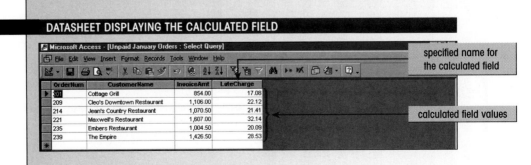

specified name for the calculated field

calculated field values

You'll save the query as Unpaid With Late Charge, and then close it.

8. Click **File** on the menu bar, click **Save As**, type **Unpaid With Late Charge**, press the **Enter** key, and then click the **Close** button ☒ on the menu bar. The Database window becomes the active window.

Barbara prepares a report of Valle Coffee's restaurant business for Leonard on a regular basis. The information in the report includes a summary of the restaurant orders. Barbara lists the total invoice amount for all orders, the average invoice amount, and the total number of orders. She asks you to create a query to determine these statistics from data in the Order table.

Using Aggregate Functions

You can calculate statistical information, such as totals and averages, on the records selected in a query. To do this, you use the Access aggregate functions. **Aggregate functions** perform arithmetic operations on selected records in a database. Figure 3-34 lists the most frequently used aggregate functions. Aggregate functions operate on the records that meet a query's selection criteria. You specify an aggregate function for a specific field, and the appropriate operation applies to that field's values for the selected records.

Figure 3-34	FREQUENTLY USED AGGREGATE FUNCTIONS	
AGGREGATE FUNCTION	**DETERMINES**	**DATA TYPES SUPPORTED**
Avg	Average of the field values for the selected records	AutoNumber, Currency, Date/Time, Number
Count	Number of records selected	AutoNumber, Currency, Date/Time, Memo, Number, OLE Object, Text, Yes/No
Max	Highest field value for the selected records	AutoNumber, Currency, Date/Time, Number, Text
Min	Lowest field value for the selected records	AutoNumber, Currency, Date/Time, Number, Text
Sum	Total of the field values for the selected records	AutoNumber, Currency, Date/Time, Number

To display the total, average, and count of all the invoice amounts in the Order table, you will use the Sum, Avg, and Count aggregate functions for the InvoiceAmt field.

To calculate the total, average, and count of all invoice amounts:

1. Double-click **Create query in Design view**. Access opens the Show Table dialog box on top of the Query window in Design view.

2. Click **Order**, click the **Add** button, and then click the **Close** button. The Order field list is added to the top of the Query window, and the dialog box closes.

To perform the three calculations on the InvoiceAmt field, you need to add the field to the design grid three times.

3. Double-click **InvoiceAmt** in the Order field list three times to add three copies of the field to the design grid.

You need to select an aggregate function for each InvoiceAmt field. When you click the Totals button on the Query Design toolbar, a row labeled "Total" is added to the design grid. The Total row provides a list of the aggregate functions that you can select.

4. Click the **Totals** button Σ on the Query Design toolbar. A new row labeled "Total" appears between the Table and Sort rows in the design grid. See Figure 3-35.

Figure 3-35	TOTAL ROW INSERTED IN THE DESIGN GRID

Totals button

Total row

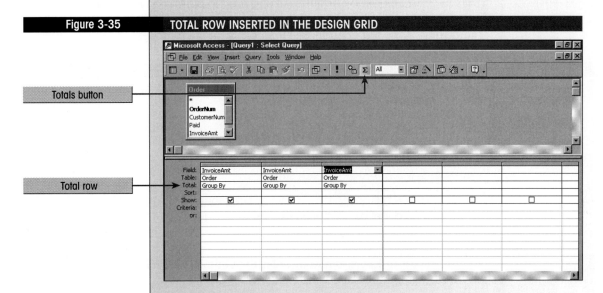

In the Total row, you specify the aggregate function you want to use for a field.

5. Click the right side of the first column's **Total** text box, and then click **Sum**. This field will calculate the total of all the InvoiceAmt field values.

When you run the query, Access automatically will assign a datasheet column name of "SumOfInvoiceAmt" for this field. You can change the datasheet column name to a more descriptive or readable name by entering the name you want in the Field text box. However, you must also keep the field name InvoiceAmt in the Field text box, because it identifies the field whose values will be summed. The Field text box will contain the datasheet column name you specify followed by the field name (InvoiceAmt) with a colon separating the two names.

6. Position the insertion point to the left of InvoiceAmt in the first column's Field text box, and then type **Total of Invoices:**. Be sure you include the colon at the end.

7. Click the right side of the second column's **Total** text box, and then click **Avg**. This field will calculate the average of all the InvoiceAmt field values.

8. Position the insertion point to the left of InvoiceAmt in the second column's Field text box, and then type **Average of Invoices:**.

9. Click the right side of the third column's **Total** text box, and then click **Count**. This field will calculate the total number of invoices (orders).

10. Position the insertion point to the left of InvoiceAmt in the third column's Field text box, and then type **Number of Invoices:**.

The query design is complete, so you can run the query.

11. Click the **Run** button [!] on the Query Design toolbar. Access runs the query and displays one record containing the three aggregate function values. The single row of summary statistics represents calculations based on the 104 records selected in the query.

You need to resize the three columns to their best fit to see the column names.

12. Resize each column by double-clicking the ✛ pointer on the right edge of each column's field selector; then position the insertion point at the start of the field value in the first column. See Figure 3-36.

Figure 3-36	RESULTS OF THE QUERY USING AGGREGATE FUNCTIONS

You'll save the query as Invoice Statistics.

13. Click the **Save** button [💾] on the Query Datasheet toolbar, type **Invoice Statistics**, and then press the **Enter** key.

Barbara's report to Leonard also includes the same invoice statistics (total, average, and count) for each month. Because Valle Coffee sends invoices to its restaurant customers once a month, each invoice in a month has the same billing date. Barbara asks you to display the invoice statistics for each different billing date in the Order table.

Using Record Group Calculations

In addition to calculating statistical information on all or selected records in selected tables, you can calculate statistics for groups of records. For example, you can determine the number of customers in each state or the total invoice amounts by billing date.

To create a query for Barbara's latest request, you can modify the current query by adding the BillingDate field and assigning the Group By operator to it. The **Group By operator** divides the selected records into groups based on the values in the specified field. Those records with the same value for the field are grouped together, and the datasheet displays one record for each group. Aggregate functions, which appear in the other columns of the design grid, provide statistical information for each group.

You need to modify the current query to add the Group By operator for the BillingDate field. This will display the statistical information grouped by billing date for the 104 selected records in the query.

To add the BillingDate field with the Group By operator, and then run the query:

1. Click the **View** button for Design view [📐] on the Query Datasheet toolbar to switch to Design view.

2. Scroll the Order field list, if necessary, and then double-click **BillingDate** to add the field to the design grid. Group By, which is the default option in the Total row, appears for the BillingDate field.

You've completed the query changes, so you can run the query.

3. Click the **Run** button [!] on the Query Design toolbar. Access runs the query and displays three records—one for each BillingDate group. Each record contains the three aggregate function values and the BillingDate field value for the group. Again, the summary statistics represent calculations based on the 104 records selected in the query. See Figure 3-37.

Figure 3-37	AGGREGATE FUNCTIONS GROUPED BY BILLINGDATE

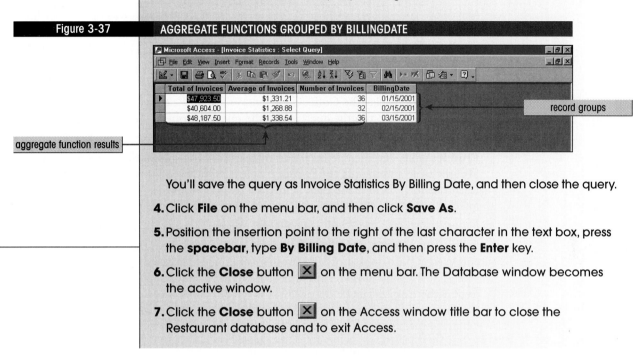

aggregate function results

record groups

You'll save the query as Invoice Statistics By Billing Date, and then close the query.

4. Click **File** on the menu bar, and then click **Save As**.

5. Position the insertion point to the right of the last character in the text box, press the **spacebar**, type **By Billing Date**, and then press the **Enter** key.

6. Click the **Close** button [X] on the menu bar. The Database window becomes the active window.

7. Click the **Close** button [X] on the Access window title bar to close the Restaurant database and to exit Access.

The queries you've created and saved will help Leonard, Barbara, Kim, and other employees monitor and analyze the business activity of Valle Coffee's restaurant customers. Now any employee can run the queries at any time, modify them as needed, or use them as the basis for designing new queries to meet additional information requirements.

Session 3.2 QUICK CHECK

1. A(n) _____ is a criterion, or rule, that determines which records are selected for a query datasheet.

2. In the design grid, where do you place the conditions for two different fields when you use the And logical operator? The Or logical operator?

3. To perform a calculation in a query, you define a(n) _____ containing a combination of database fields, constants, and operators.

4. How does a calculated field differ from a table field?

5. What is an aggregate function?

6. The _____ operator divides selected records into groups based on the values in a field.

REVIEW ASSIGNMENTS

Barbara needs information from the **Valle Products** database, and she asks you to query the database by completing the following:

1. Make sure your Data Disk is in the disk drive, start Access, and then open the **Valle Products** database located in the Review folder on your Data Disk.

2. Create a select query based on the **Product** table. Display the ProductCode, WeightCode, and Price fields in the query results; sort in descending order based on the Price field values; and select only those records whose CoffeeCode value equals BRUM. (*Hint*: Do not display the CoffeeCode field values in the query results.) Save the query as **BRUM Coffee**, run the query, print the query datasheet, and then close the query.

Explore 3. Define a one-to-many relationship between the primary **Coffee** table and the related **Product** table, and then define a one-to-many relationship between the primary **Weight** table and the related **Product** table. (*Hint*: Add all three tables to the Relationships window, and then define the two relationships.) Select the referential integrity option and both cascade options for both relationships.

4. Create a select query based on the **Coffee**, **Product**, and **Weight** tables. Select the fields CoffeeType, CoffeeName, ProductCode, Decaf (from the **Product** table), Price, and Weight/Size, in that order. Sort in ascending order based on the CoffeeName field values. Select only those records whose CoffeeType equals "Flavored." (*Hint*: Do not display the CoffeeType field values in the query results.) Save the query as **Flavored Coffees**, and then run the query. Resize all columns in the datasheet to fit the data. Print the datasheet, and then save the query.

5. Use the Office Assistant to learn about Filter By Form. (*Hint:* Ask the Office Assistant the question, "How do I use Filter By Form," and then click the topic "Filter records by entering values in a blank view of your form or datasheet.") Read the topic, and then close the Microsoft Access Help window.

Explore 6. Use the Filter By Form button on the Query Datasheet toolbar to filter the records that have a Weight/Size of "1 lb pkg," and then apply the filter. Print the query datasheet.

Explore 7. Remove the filter to display all records, and then save and close the query.

Explore 8. Create a query based on the **Product** table that shows all products that do not have a WeightCode field value of A, and whose Price field value is greater than 50; display all fields except Decaf from the **Product** table. Save the query as **Pricing**, and then run the query.

Explore 9. Open the **Pricing** query in Design view. Create a calculated field named NewPrice that displays the results of increasing the Price values by 3%. Display the results in descending order by NewPrice. Save the query as **New Prices**, run the query, resize all columns in the datasheet to fit the data, print the query datasheet, and then save and close the query.

10. Open the **Flavored Coffees** query in Design view. Modify the query to display only those records with a CoffeeType field value of "Flavored" or with a Price field value greater than 50. Save the query as **Flavored Plus Higher Priced**, and then run the query. Resize all columns in the datasheet to fit the data, print the query datasheet, and then save and close the query.

Explore 11. Create a new query based on the **Product** table. Use the Min and Max aggregate functions to find the lowest and highest values in the Price field. Name the two aggregate fields Lowest Price and Highest Price, respectively. Save the query as **Lowest And Highest Prices**, run the query, and then print the query datasheet.

Explore 12. Open the **Lowest And Highest Prices** query in Design view. Use the Show Table button on the Query Design toolbar to open the Show Table dialog box, and then add the **Weight** table to the query. Modify the query so that the records are grouped by the Weight/Size field. Save the query as **Lowest And Highest Prices By Weight/Size**, run the query, print the query datasheet, and then close the query.

13. Close the **Valle Products** database, and then exit Access.

CASE PROBLEMS

Case 1. Ashbrook Mall Information Desk   Sam Bullard wants to view specific information about jobs available at the Ashbrook Mall. He asks you to query the **MallJobs** database by completing the following:

1. Make sure your Data Disk is in the disk drive, start Access, and then open the **MallJobs** database located in the Cases folder on your Data Disk.

2. Define a one-to-many relationship between the primary **Store** table and the related **Job** table. Select the referential integrity option and both cascade options for the relationship.

3. Create a select query based on the **Store** and **Job** tables. Display the StoreName, Location, Position, and Hours/Week fields, in that order. Sort in ascending order based on the StoreName field values. Run the query, save the query as **Store Jobs**, and then print the datasheet.

4. Use Filter By Selection to temporarily display only those records with a Location field value of A3 in the **Store Jobs** query datasheet. Print the datasheet and then remove the filter. Save and close the query.

5. Open the **Store Jobs** query in Design view. Modify the query to display only those records with a Position value of Server. Run the query, save the query as **Server Jobs**, and then print the datasheet.

6. Open the **Server Jobs** query in Design view. Modify the query to display only those records with a Position value of Server and with an Hours/Week value of 20-25. Run the query, save it with the same name, print the datasheet, and then close the query.

7. Close the **MallJobs** database, and then exit Access.

Case 2. Professional Litigation User Services (PLUS)   Raj Jawahir is completing an analysis of the payment history of PLUS clients. To help him find the information he needs, you'll query the **Payments** database by completing the following:

1. Make sure your Data Disk is in the disk drive, start Access, and then open the **Payments** database located in the Cases folder on your Data Disk.

2. Define a one-to-many relationship between the primary **Firm** table and the related **Payment** table. Select the referential integrity option and both cascade options for the relationship.

3. Create a select query based on the **Firm** and **Payment** tables. Display the fields Firm# (from the **Firm** table), FirmName, AmtPaid, and DatePaid, in that order. Sort in descending order based on the AmtPaid field values. Select only those records whose AmtPaid is greater than 2500. Save the query as **Large Payments**, and then run the query. Print the datasheet and then close the query.

4. For all payments on 06/01/2001, display the Payment#, AmtPaid, DatePaid, and FirmName fields. Save the query as **June 1 Payments**, and then run the query. Switch to Design view, modify the query so that the DatePaid values do not appear in the query results, and then save the modified query. Run the query, print the query results, and then close the query.

Explore 5. For all firms that have Olivia Tyler as a PLUS account representative, display the FirmName, FirmContact, AmtPaid, and DatePaid fields. Save the query as **Tyler Accounts**, run the query, print the query results, and then close the query.

6. For all payments made on 06/10/2001 or 06/11/2001, display the fields DatePaid, AmtPaid, FirmName, and Firm# (from the **Firm** table). Display the results in ascending order by DatePaid and then in descending order by AmtPaid. Save the query as **Selected Dates**, run the query, print the query datasheet, and then close the query.

Explore 7. Use the **Payment** table to display the highest, lowest, total, average, and count of the AmtPaid field for all payments. Then do the following:

   a. Specify column names of HighestPayment, LowestPayment, TotalPayments, AveragePayment, and #Payments. Save the query as **Payment Statistics**, and then run the query. Resize all datasheet columns to their best fit, save the query, and then print the query results.

   b. Change the query to display the same statistics grouped by DatePaid. Save the query as **Payment Statistics By Date**, run the query, and then print the query results.

   c. Change the **Payment Statistics By Date** query to display the same statistics by DatePaid, then by Deposit#. Save the query as **Payment Statistics By Date By Deposit**, run the query, print the query results using landscape orientation, and then save and close the query.

8. Close the **Payments** database, and then exit Access.

Case 3. Best Friends   Noah and Sheila Warnick want to find specific information about the walk-a-thons they conduct for Best Friends. You'll help them find the information in the **Walks** database by completing the following:

1. Make sure your Data Disk is in the disk drive, start Access, and then open the **Walks** database located in the Cases folder on your Data Disk.

2. Define a one-to-many relationship between the primary **Walker** table and the related **Pledge** table. Select the referential integrity option and both cascade options for the relationship.

3. For all walkers with a PledgeAmt field value of greater than 30, display the WalkerID, LastName, PledgeNo, and PledgeAmt fields. Sort the query in ascending order by PledgeAmt. Save the query as **Large Pledges**, run the query, print the query datasheet, and then close the query.

4. For all walkers who pledged less than $15 or who pledged $5 per mile, display the Pledger, PledgeAmt, PerMile, LastName, FirstName, and Distance fields. Save the query as **Pledged Or Per Mile**, run the query, and then print the query datasheet. Change the query to select all walkers who pledged less than $15 and who pledged $5 per mile. Save the query as **Pledged And Per Mile**, and then run the query. Describe the results. Close the query.

Explore 5. For all pledges, display the WalkerID, Pledger, Distance, PerMile, and PledgeAmt fields. Save the query as **Difference**. Create a calculated field named CalcPledgeAmt that displays the results of multiplying the Distance and PerMile fields; then save the query. Create a second calculated field named Difference that displays the results of subtracting the CalcPledgeAmt field from the PledgeAmt field. Format the calculated fields as fixed. (*Hint*: Choose the Properties option on the shortcut menu for the selected field.) Display the results in ascending order by PledgeAmt. Save the modified query, and then run the query. Resize all datasheet columns to their best fit, print the query results, and then save and close the query.

6. Use the **Pledge** table to display the total, average, and count of the PledgeAmt field for all pledges. Then do the following:

   a. Specify column names of TotalPledge, AveragePledge, and #Pledges.

   Explore   b. Change properties so that the values in the TotalPledge and AveragePledge columns display two decimal places and the fixed format. (*Hint*: Choose the Properties option on the shortcut menu for the selected field.)

   c. Save the query as **Pledge Statistics**, run the query, resize all datasheet columns to their best fit, and then print the query datasheet. Save the query.

   Explore   d. Change the query to display the sum, average, and count of the PledgeAmt field for all pledges by LastName. (*Hint*: Use the Show Table button on the Query Design toolbar to add the **Walker** table to the query.) Save the query as **Pledge Statistics By Walker**, run the query, print the query datasheet, and then close the query.

7. Close the **Walks** database, and then exit Access.

Case 4. Lopez Lexus Dealerships   Maria and Hector Lopez want to analyze data about the cars and different locations for their Lexus dealerships. Help them query the **Lexus** database by completing the following:

1. Make sure your Data Disk is in the disk drive, start Access, and then open the **Lexus** database located in the Cases folder on your Data Disk.

2. Define a one-to-many relationship between the primary **Locations** table and the related **Cars** table. Select the referential integrity option and both cascade options for the relationship.

3. For all vehicles, display the Model, Class, Year, LocationCode, and SellingPrice fields. Save the query as **Car Info**, and then run the query. Resize all datasheet columns to their best fit. In Datasheet view, sort the query results in descending order by the SellingPrice field. Print the query datasheet, and then save and close the query.

4. For all vehicles manufactured in 2000, display the Model, Year, Cost, SellingPrice, and LocationName fields. Sort the query in ascending order by Cost. Save the query as **2000 Cars**, and then run the query. Modify the query to remove the display of the Year field values from the query results. Save the modified query, run the query, print the query datasheet, and then close the query.

Explore   5. For all vehicles located in Laredo or with a transmission of M5, display the Model, Year, Cost, SellingPrice, Transmission, LocationCode, and LocationName fields. Save the query as **Location Or Trans**, run the query, and then print the query datasheet using landscape orientation. Change the query to select all vehicles located in Laredo and with a transmission of M5. Save the query as **Location And Trans**, run the query, print the query datasheet in landscape orientation, and then close the query.

6. For all vehicles, display the Model, Class, Year, Cost, and SellingPrice fields. Save the query as **Profit**. Then create a calculated field named Profit that displays the difference between the vehicle's selling price and cost. Display the results in descending order by Profit. Save the query, run the query, print the query datasheet, and then close the query.

Explore   7. Use the **Cars** table to determine the total cost, average cost, total selling price, and average selling price of all vehicles. Use the Index tab in online Help to look up the word "caption"; then click the topic "Change a field name in a query." Read the displayed information, and then click and read the subtopic "Display new field names by changing the Caption property." Close the Help window. Set the Caption property of the four fields to Total Cost, Average Cost, Total Selling Price, and Average Selling Price, respectively. Save the query as **Car Statistics**, run the query, resize all datasheet columns to their best fit, print the query datasheet, and then save the query again. Revise the query to show the car statistics grouped by LocationName. (*Hint*: Use the Show Table button on the Query Design toolbar to display the Show Table dialog box.) Set the Caption property of the LocationName field to Location. Save the revised query as **Car Statistics By Location**, run the query, print the query datasheet, and then close the query.

Explore   8. Use the Answer Wizard to ask the following question: "How do I create a Top Values query?" Click the topic "Display only the highest or lowest values in the query's results." Read the displayed information, and then close the Help window. Open the **Profit** query in Design view, and then modify the query to display only the top five values for the Profit field. Save the query as **Top Profit**, run the query, print the query datasheet, and then close the query.

9. Close the **Lexus** database, and then exit Access.

INTERNET ASSIGNMENTS

The purpose of the Internet Assignments is to challenge you to find information on the Internet that you can use to create effective documents. The actual assignments are updated and maintained on the Course Technology Web site. Log on to the Internet and use your Web browser to go to the Student Online Companion to accompany this text at **www.course.com/NewPerspectives/office2000**. Click the Access link, and then click the link for Tutorial 3.

QUICK CHECK ANSWERS

Session 3.1

1. a general query in which you specify the fields and records you want Access to select
2. The field list contains the table name at the top of the list box and the table's fields listed in the order in which they appear in the table; the design grid displays columns that contain specifications about a field you will use in the query.
3. A table datasheet and a query datasheet look the same, appearing in Datasheet view, and can be used to update data in a database. A table datasheet shows the permanent data in a table, whereas a query datasheet is temporary and its contents are based on the criteria you establish in the design grid.
4. primary table; related table
5. referential integrity
6. oldest to most recent date
7. when you want to perform different types of sorts (both ascending and descending, for example) on multiple fields, and when you want to sort on multiple fields that are nonadjacent or in the wrong order, but you do not want to rearrange the columns in the query datasheet to accomplish the sort
8. filter

Session 3.2

1. condition
2. in the same Criteria row; in different Criteria rows
3. expression
4. A calculated field appears in a query datasheet but does not exist in a database, as does a table field.
5. a function that performs an arithmetic operation on selected records in a database
6. Group By

In this tutorial you will:

- Create a form using the Form Wizard

- Change a form's AutoFormat

- Navigate a form and find data using a form

- Preview and print selected form records

- Maintain table data using a form

- Create a form with a main form and a subform

- Create a report using the Report Wizard

- Insert a picture in a report

- Preview and print a report

CREATING FORMS AND REPORTS

Creating an Order Data Form, a Customer Orders Form, and a Customers and Orders Report

CASE

Valle Coffee

Barbara Hennessey wants to continue to enhance the Restaurant database to make it easier for her office staff members and other Valle Coffee employees to find and maintain data. In particular, she wants the database to include a form for the Order table, similar to the Customer Data form, which is based on the Customer table. She also wants a form that shows data from both the Customer and Order tables at the same time, so that all the order information for each customer appears with the corresponding customer data, giving a complete picture of the restaurant customers and their orders.

In addition, Kim Carpenter would like a report showing customer and order data, so that her marketing staff members will have printed output to refer to when completing market analyses and planning strategies for selling to restaurant customers. She wants the information to be formatted attractively, perhaps including the Valle Coffee cup logo on the report for visual interest.

**SESSION
4.1**

In this session, you will create a form using the Form Wizard, change a form's AutoFormat, navigate a form, find data using a form, preview and print selected form records, and maintain table data using a form.

Creating a Form Using the Form Wizard

As you learned in Tutorial 1, a form is an object you use to maintain, view, and print records in a database. In Access, you can design your own forms or use Form Wizards to create them for you automatically.

Barbara asks you to create a new form that her staff can use to view and maintain data in the Order table. In Tutorial 1, you used the AutoForm Wizard—which creates a form automatically, using all the fields in the selected table or query—to create the Customer Data form. To create the form for the Order table, you'll use the Form Wizard. The **Form Wizard** allows you to choose some or all of the fields in the selected table or query, choose fields from other tables and queries, and display the chosen fields in any order on the form. You can also choose a style for the form.

> ### To open the Restaurant database and activate the Form Wizard:
>
> 1. Place your Data Disk in the appropriate disk drive.
>
> 2. Start Access and open the Restaurant database located in the Tutorial folder on your Data Disk. The Restaurant database is displayed in the Access window.
>
> 3. Click **Forms** in the Objects bar of the Database window. The Forms list includes the Customer Data form you created in Tutorial 1.
>
> 4. Click the **New** button in the Database window. The New Form dialog box opens.
>
> 5. Click **Form Wizard**, click the list arrow for choosing a table or query, click **Order** to select this table as the source for the form, and then click the **OK** button. The first Form Wizard dialog box opens. See Figure 4-1.

Figure 4-1	FIRST FORM WIZARD DIALOG BOX

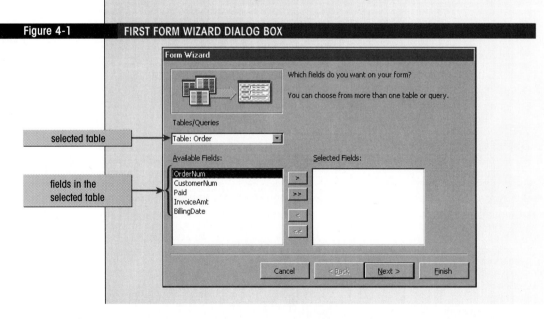

Barbara wants the form to display all the fields in the Order table, but in a different order. She would like the Paid field to appear at the bottom of the form so that it stands out more, making it easier to determine if an order has been paid.

To finish creating the form using the Form Wizard:

1. Click **OrderNum** in the Available Fields list box (if necessary), and then click the ⊳ button to move the field to the Selected Fields list box.

2. Repeat Step 1 to select the **CustomerNum**, **InvoiceAmt**, **BillingDate**, and **Paid** fields, in that order.

3. Click the **Next** button to display the second Form Wizard dialog box, in which you select a layout for the form. See Figure 4-2.

Figure 4-2	CHOOSING A LAYOUT FOR THE FORM

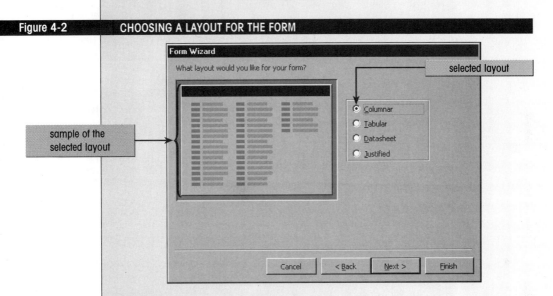

The layout choices are columnar, tabular, datasheet, and justified. A sample of the selected layout appears on the left side of the dialog box.

4. Click each of the option buttons and review the corresponding sample layout.

The tabular and datasheet layouts display the fields from multiple records at one time, whereas the columnar and justified layouts display the fields from one record at a time. Barbara thinks the columnar layout is the appropriate arrangement for displaying and updating data in the table, so you'll choose this layout.

5. Click the **Columnar** option button (if necessary), and then click the **Next** button. Access displays the third Form Wizard dialog box, in which you choose a style for the form. See Figure 4-3.

Figure 4-3	CHOOSING A STYLE FOR THE FORM

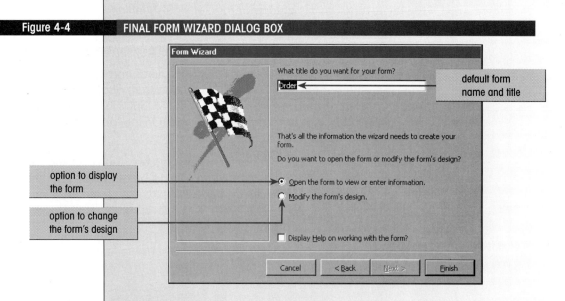

A sample of the selected style appears in the box on the left. If you choose a style, which is called an **AutoFormat**, and decide you'd prefer a different one after the form is created, you can change it.

TROUBLE? Don't worry if a different form style is selected in your dialog box than the one shown in Figure 4-3. The dialog box displays the most recently used style, which might be different on your computer.

6. Click each of the styles and review the corresponding sample.

Barbara likes the Expedition style and asks you to use it for the form.

7. Click **Expedition** and then click the **Next** button. Access displays the final Form Wizard dialog box and shows the Order table's name as the default form name; "Order" is also the default title that will appear in the form's title bar. See Figure 4-4.

Figure 4-4	FINAL FORM WIZARD DIALOG BOX

You'll use Order Data as the form name and, because you don't need to change the form's design at this point, you'll display the form.

8. Position the insertion point to the right of Order in the text box, press the **spacebar**, type **Data**, and then click the **Finish** button. The completed form is displayed in Form view. See Figure 4-5.

Figure 4-5	COMPLETED FORM FOR THE ORDER TABLE

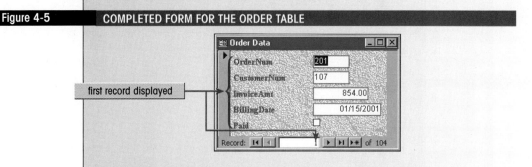

first record displayed

TROUBLE? If the navigation bar at the bottom of your Form window does not display all of the navigation buttons or the "of 104" text, drag the right edge of the Form window to the right so that all of the navigation bar is visible.

After viewing the form, Barbara decides that she doesn't like the form's style—the background makes the field names a bit difficult to read. She asks you to change the form's style.

Changing a Form's AutoFormat

You can change a form's appearance by choosing a different AutoFormat for the form. As you learned when you created the Order Data form, an **AutoFormat** is a predefined style for a form (or report). The AutoFormats available for a form are the ones you saw when you selected the form's style using the Form Wizard. To change an AutoFormat, you must switch to Design view.

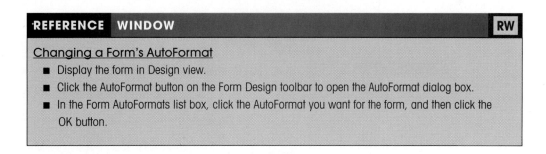

REFERENCE WINDOW	RW

Changing a Form's AutoFormat
- Display the form in Design view.
- Click the AutoFormat button on the Form Design toolbar to open the AutoFormat dialog box.
- In the Form AutoFormats list box, click the AutoFormat you want for the form, and then click the OK button.

To change the AutoFormat for the Order Data form:

1. Click the **View** button for Design view 🖾 on the Form View toolbar. The form is displayed in Design view. See Figure 4-6.

Figure 4-6   FORM DISPLAYED IN DESIGN VIEW

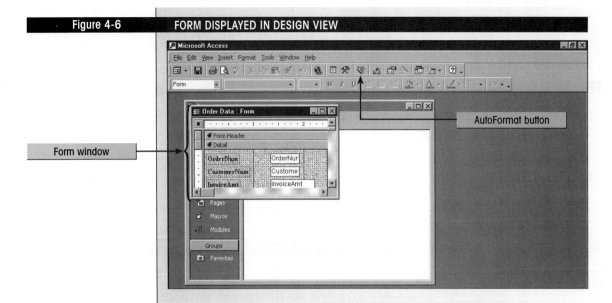

TROUBLE? If your screen displays any window other than those shown in Figure 4-6, click the Close button [X] on the window's title bar to close it.

You use Design view to modify an existing form or to create a form from scratch. In this case, you need to change the AutoFormat for the Order Data form.

2. Click the **AutoFormat** button 🖳 on the Form Design toolbar. The AutoFormat dialog box opens.

3. Click the **Options** button to display the AutoFormat options. See Figure 4-7.

Figure 4-7   AUTOFORMAT DIALOG BOX

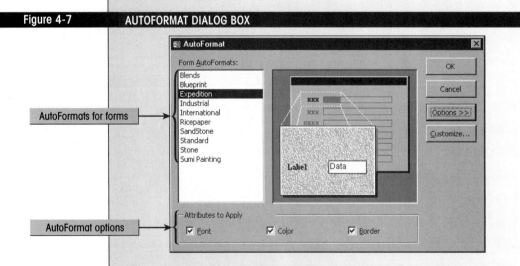

A sample of the selected AutoFormat appears to the right of the Form AutoFormats list box. The options at the bottom of the dialog box allow you to apply the selected AutoFormat or just its font, color, or border.

Barbara decides that she prefers the Standard AutoFormat, because its field names and field values are easy to read.

4. Click **Standard** in the Form AutoFormats list box, and then click the **OK** button. The AutoFormat dialog box closes, the Standard AutoFormat is applied to the form, and the Form window in Design view becomes the active window.

5. Click the **View** button for Form view 🔳 on the Form Design toolbar. The form is displayed in Form view with the new AutoFormat. See Figure 4-8.

Figure 4-8	FORM DISPLAYED WITH THE NEW AUTOFORMAT

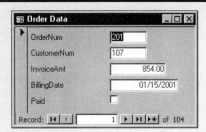

You have finished modifying the format of the form and can now save it.

6. Click the **Save** button 🖫 on the Form View toolbar to save the modified form.

Barbara wants to view some data in the Order table, using the form. To view data, you need to navigate through the form.

Navigating a Form

To maintain and view data using a form, you must know how to move from field to field and from record to record. The mouse movement, selection, and placement techniques to navigate a form are the same techniques you've used to navigate a table datasheet and the Customer Data form you created in Tutorial 1. Also, the navigation mode and editing mode keystroke techniques are the same as those you used previously for datasheets (see Figure 2-31).

To navigate through the form:

1. Press the **Tab** key to move to the CustomerNum field value, and then press the **End** key to move to the Paid field. Because the Paid field is a yes/no field, its value is not highlighted; instead, a dashed box appears around the field name to indicate that it is the current field.

2. Press the **Home** key to move back to the OrderNum field value. The first record in the Order table still appears in the form.

3. Press **Ctrl + End** to move to the Paid field in record 104, which is the last record in the table. The record number for the current record appears between the navigation buttons at the bottom of the form.

4. Click the **Previous Record** navigation button ◄ to move to the Paid field in record 103.

5. Press the ↑ key twice to move to the InvoiceAmt field value in record 103.

6. Position the insertion point between the numbers "2" and "6" in the InvoiceAmt field value to switch to editing mode, press the **Home** key to move the insertion point to the beginning of the field value, and then press the **End** key to move the insertion point to the end of the field value.

7. Click the **First Record** navigation button [◄] to move to the InvoiceAmt field value in the first record. The entire field value is highlighted because you have switched from editing mode to navigation mode.

8. Click the **Next Record** navigation button [▶] to move to the InvoiceAmt field value in record 2, which is the next record.

Barbara asks you to display the records for Jean's Country Restaurant, whose customer number is 407, because she wants to review the orders for this customer.

Finding Data Using a Form

The **Find** command allows you to search the data in a form and to display only those records you want to view. You choose a field to serve as the basis for the search by making that field the current field; then you enter the value you want Access to match in the Find and Replace dialog box. You can use the Find command for a form or datasheet, and you can activate the command from the Edit menu or by clicking the toolbar Find button.

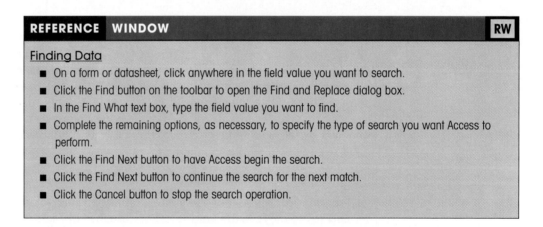

REFERENCE	WINDOW	RW

Finding Data
- On a form or datasheet, click anywhere in the field value you want to search.
- Click the Find button on the toolbar to open the Find and Replace dialog box.
- In the Find What text box, type the field value you want to find.
- Complete the remaining options, as necessary, to specify the type of search you want Access to perform.
- Click the Find Next button to have Access begin the search.
- Click the Find Next button to continue the search for the next match.
- Click the Cancel button to stop the search operation.

You need to find all records in the Order table for Jean's Country Restaurant, whose customer number is 407.

To find the records using the Order Data form:

1. Position the insertion point in the CustomerNum field value box. This is the field for which you will find matching values.

2. Click the **Find** button [🔍] on the Form View toolbar. The Find and Replace dialog box opens. Note that the Look In list box shows the name of the field that Access will search (in this case, the CustomerNum field), and the Match list box indicates that Access will find values that match the entire entry in the field. You could choose to match only part of a field value.

3. If the Find and Replace dialog box covers any part of the form, move the dialog box by dragging its title bar. Move the Order Data form window as well, if necessary. See Figure 4-9.

| Figure 4-9 | FIND AND REPLACE DIALOG BOX |

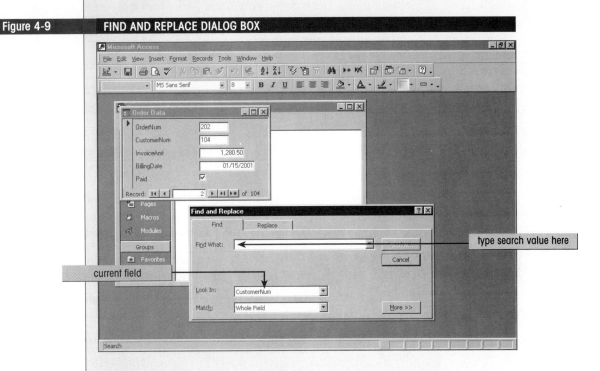

4. In the Find What text box, type **407** and then click the **Find Next** button. Access displays record 14, which is the first record for CustomerNum 407.

5. Click the **Find Next** button. Access displays record 51, which is the second record for CustomerNum 407.

6. Click the **Find Next** button. Access displays record 88, which is the third record for CustomerNum 407.

7. Click the **Find Next** button. Access displays a dialog box informing you that the search is finished.

8. Click the **OK** button to close the dialog box.

The search value you enter can be an exact value, such as the customer number 407 you just entered, or it can include wildcard characters. A **wildcard character** is a placeholder you use when you know only part of a value or when you want to start or end with a specific character or match a certain pattern. Figure 4-10 shows the wildcard characters you can use when finding data.

Figure 4-10	WILDCARD CHARACTERS	
WILDCARD CHARACTER	**PURPOSE**	**EXAMPLE**
*	Match any number of characters. It can be used as the first and/or last character in the character string.	th* finds *the, that, this, therefore,* and so on
?	Match any single alphabetic character.	a?t finds *act, aft, ant,* and *art*
[ ]	Match any single character within the brackets.	a[fr]t finds *aft* and *art* but not *act* and *ant*
!	Match any character not within brackets.	a[!fr]t finds *act* and *ant* but not *aft* and *art*
-	Match any one of a range of characters. The range must be in ascending order (a to z, not z to a).	a[d-p]t finds *aft* and *ant* but not *act* and *art*
#	Match any single numeric character.	#72 finds *072, 172, 272, 372,* and so on

To check if their orders have been paid, Barbara wants to view the order records for two customers: Cheshire Restaurant (CustomerNum 515) and Around the Clock Restaurant (CustomerNum 597). You'll use the * wildcard character to search for these customers' orders.

To find the records using the * wildcard character:

1. Double-click **407** in the Find What text box to select the entire value, and then type **5***.

   Access will match any field value in the CustomerNum field that starts with the digit 5.

2. Click the **Find Next** button. Access displays record 16, which is the first record for CustomerNum 515. Note that the Paid field value is checked, indicating that this order has been paid.

3. Click the **Find Next** button. Access displays record 17, which is the first record for CustomerNum 597.

4. Click the **Find Next** button. Access displays record 39, which is the second record for CustomerNum 597.

5. Click the **Find Next** button. Access displays record 68, which is the second record for CustomerNum 515.

6. Click the **Find Next** button. Access displays record 82, which is the third record for CustomerNum 515.

7. Click the **Find Next** button. Access displays a dialog box informing you that the search is finished.

8. Click the **OK** button to close the dialog box.

9. Click the **Cancel** button to close the Find and Replace dialog box.

All five orders have been paid, but Barbara wants to make sure Valle Coffee has a record of payment for order number 375. She asks you to print the data displayed on the form for record 82, which is for order number 375, so she can ask a staff member to look for the payment record for this order.

Previewing and Printing Selected Form Records

Access prints as many form records as can fit on a printed page. If only part of a form record fits on the bottom of a page, the remainder of the record prints on the next page. Access allows you to print all pages or a range of pages. In addition, you can print the currently selected form record.

Before printing record 82, you'll preview the form record to see how it will look when printed.

To preview the form and print the data for record 82:

1. Make sure record 82 is the current record in the Order Data form.

2. Click the **Print Preview** button 🔍 on the Form View toolbar. The Print Preview window opens, showing the form records for the Order table in miniature.

3. Click the **Maximize** button ☐ on the form's title bar.

4. Click the **Zoom** button 🔍 on the Print Preview toolbar, and then use the vertical scroll bar to view the contents of the window. See Figure 4-11.

| Figure 4-11 | PRINT PREVIEW WINDOW DISPLAYING FORM RECORDS |

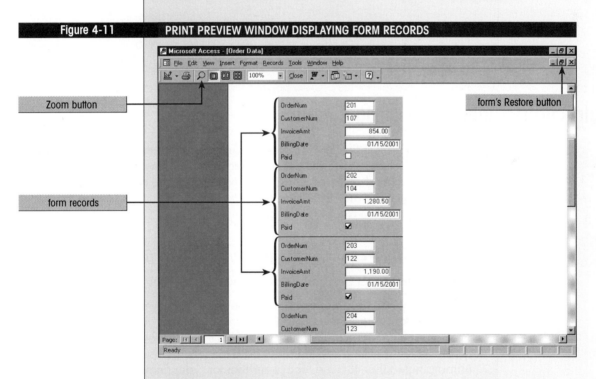

TROUBLE? The field labels in your form might be truncated so that all letters do not display correctly. This problem will not affect the steps; continue with Step 5.

Each record from the Order table appears in a separate form. Access places as many form records as will fit on each page.

5. Click the **Restore** button 🗗 on the Print Preview menu bar, and then click the **Close** button on the Print Preview toolbar to return to the table in Form view.

6. Click **File** on the menu bar, and then click **Print**. The Print dialog box opens.

7. Click the **Selected Record(s)** option button to print only the current form record (record 82).

8. Click the **OK** button to close the dialog box and to print the selected record.

Barbara has identified several updates she wants you to make to the Order table using the Order Data form, as shown in Figure 4-12.

Figure 4-12	UPDATES TO THE ORDER TABLE

Order Number	Update Action
319	Change InvoiceAmt to 1,175.00 Change Paid to Yes
392	Delete record
400	Add new record for CustomerNum 135, InvoiceAmt of 1,350.00, BillingDate of 03/15/2001, and Paid status of No

Maintaining Table Data Using a Form

Maintaining data using a form is often easier than using a datasheet, because you can concentrate on all the changes required to a single record at one time. You already know how to navigate a form and find specific records. Now you'll make the changes Barbara requested to the Order table, using the Order Data form.

First, you'll update the record for OrderNum 319.

To change the record using the Order Data form:

1. Make sure the Order Data form is displayed in Form view.

The current record number appears between the sets of navigation buttons at the bottom of the form. If you know the number of the record you want to change, you can type the number and press the Enter key to go directly to the record. When she reviewed the order data to identify possible corrections, Barbara noted that 48 is the record number for order number 319.

2. Select the number **82** that appears between the navigation buttons, type **48**, and then press the **Enter** key. Record 48 (order number 319) is now the current record.

You need to change the InvoiceAmt field value to 1,175.00 and the Paid field value to Yes for this record.

3. Position the insertion point between the numbers 9 and 5 in the InvoiceAmt field value, press the **Backspace** key, and then type **7**. Note that the pencil symbol appears in the top left of the form, indicating that the form is in editing mode.

4. Press the **Tab** key twice to move to the Paid field value, and then press the **spacebar** to insert a check mark in the check box. See Figure 4-13.

Figure 4-13	ORDER RECORD AFTER CHANGING FIELD VALUES

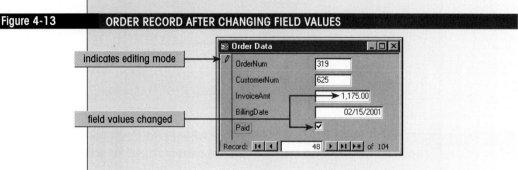

indicates editing mode

field values changed

You have completed the changes for order number 319. Barbara's next update is to delete the record for order number 392. The customer who placed this order canceled it before the order was filled and processed.

To delete the record using the Order Data form:

1. Click anywhere in the OrderNum field value to make it the current field.

2. Click the **Find** button 🔍 on the Form View toolbar. The Find and Replace dialog box opens.

3. Type **392** in the Find What text box, click the **Find Next** button, and then click the **Cancel** button. The record for order number 392 is now the current record.

4. Click the **Delete Record** button ▶🗙 on the Form View toolbar. A dialog box opens, asking you to confirm the record deletion.

5. Click the **Yes** button. The dialog box closes, and the record for order number 392 is deleted from the table.

Barbara's final maintenance change is to add a record for a new order placed by Topview Restaurant.

To add the new record using the Order Data form:

1. Click the **New Record** button ▶❋ on the Form View toolbar. Record 104, the next record available for a new record, becomes the current record. All field value boxes are empty, and the insertion point is positioned at the beginning of the field value for OrderNum.

2. Refer to Figure 4-14 and enter the value shown for each field. Press the **Tab** key to move from field to field.

Figure 4-14	COMPLETED FORM FOR THE NEW RECORD.

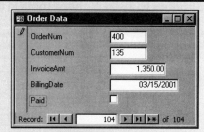

TROUBLE? Compare your screen with Figure 4-14. If any field value is wrong, correct it now, using the methods described earlier for editing field values.

3. After entering the value for BillingDate, press the **Tab** key twice (if necessary). Record 105, the next record available for a new record, becomes the current record, and the record for order number 400 is saved in the Order table.

You've completed Barbara's changes to the Order table, so you can close the Order Data form.

4. Click the **Close** button ☒ on the form's title bar. The form closes and you return to the Database window. Notice that the Order Data form is listed in the Forms list box.

The Order Data form will enable Barbara and her staff to enter and maintain data easily in the Order table. In the next session, you'll create another form for working with data in both the Order and Customer tables at the same time. You'll also create a report showing data from both tables.

Session 4.1 QUICK CHECK

1. Describe the difference between creating a form using the AutoForm Wizard and creating a form using the Form Wizard.

2. What is an AutoFormat, and how do you change one for an existing form?

3. Which table record is displayed in a form when you press Ctrl + End while you are in navigation mode?

4. You can use the Find command to search for data in a form or _____.

5. Which wildcard character matches any single alphabetic character?

6. How many form records does Access print by default on a page?

SESSION 4.2

In this session, you will create a form with a main form and a subform, create a report using the Report Wizard, insert a picture in a report, and preview and print a report.

Barbara would like you to create a form so that she can view the data for each customer and all the orders for the customer at the same time. The type of form you need to create will include a main form and a subform.

Creating a Form with a Main Form and a Subform

To create a form based on two tables, you must first define a relationship between the two tables. In Tutorial 3, you defined a one-to-many relationship between the Customer (primary) and Order (related) tables, so you are ready to create the form based on both tables.

When you create a form containing data from two tables that have a one-to-many relationship, you actually create a main form for data from the primary table and a subform for data from the related table. Access uses the defined relationship between the tables to automatically join the tables through the common field that exists in both tables.

Barbara and her staff will use the form when contacting customers about the status of their order payments. Consequently, the main form will contain the customer number and name, owner name, and phone number; the subform will contain the order number, paid status, invoice amount, and billing date.

You'll use the Form Wizard to create the form.

To create the form using the Form Wizard:

1. If you took a break after the previous session, make sure that Access is running and the Restaurant database is open.

2. Make sure the Forms object is selected in the Database window, and then click the **New** button. The New Form dialog box opens.

   When creating a form based on two tables, you first choose the primary table and select the fields you want to include in the main form; then you choose the related table and select fields from it for the subform.

3. Click **Form Wizard**, click the list arrow for choosing a table or query, click **Customer** to select this table as the source for the main form, and then click the **OK** button. The first Form Wizard dialog box opens, in which you select fields in the order you want them to appear on the main form.

   Barbara wants the form to include only the CustomerNum, CustomerName, OwnerName, and Phone fields from the Customer table.

4. Click **CustomerNum** in the Available Fields list box (if necessary), and then click the [>] button to move the field to the Selected Fields list box.

5. Repeat Step 4 for the **CustomerName**, **OwnerName**, and **Phone** fields.

   The CustomerNum field will appear in the main form, so you do not have to include it in the subform. Otherwise, Barbara wants the subform to include all the fields from the Order table.

6. Click the **Tables/Queries** list arrow, and then click **Table: Order**. The fields from the Order table appear in the Available Fields list box. The quickest way to add the fields you want to include is to move all the fields to the Selected Fields list box, and then to remove the only field you don't want to include (CustomerNum).

7. Click the ⟩⟩ button to move all the fields from the Order table to the Selected Fields list box.

8. Click **Order.CustomerNum** in the Selected Fields list box, and then click the ⟨ button to move the field back to the Available Fields list box. Note that the table name (Order) is included in the field name to distinguish it from the same field (CustomerNum) in the Customer table.

9. Click the **Next** button. The next Form Wizard dialog box opens. See Figure 4-15.

Figure 4-15   **CHOOSING A MAIN/SUBFORM FORMAT**

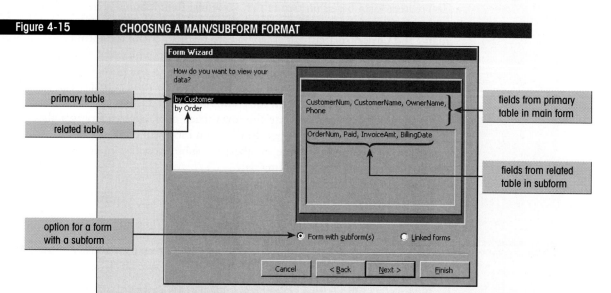

In this dialog box, the list box on the left shows the order in which you will view the selected data: first by data from the Customer table (primary table), then by data from the Order table (related table). The form will be displayed as shown in the right side of the dialog box, with the fields from the Customer table at the top in the main form, and the fields from the Order table at the bottom in the subform. The selected option button specifies a main form with a subform.

The default options shown in Figure 4-15 are correct for creating a form with Customer data in the main form and Order data in the subform.

To finish creating the form:

1. Click the **Next** button. The next Form Wizard dialog box opens, in which you choose the subform layout.

The tabular layout displays subform fields as a table, whereas the datasheet layout displays subform fields as a table datasheet. The layout choice is a matter of personal preference. You'll use the datasheet layout.

2. Click the **Datasheet** option button (if necessary), and then click the **Next** button. The next Form Wizard dialog box opens, in which you choose the form's style.

   Barbara wants all forms to have the same style, so you will choose Standard, which is the same style you used to create the Order Data form earlier.

3. Click **Standard** (if necessary) and then click the **Next** button. The next Form Wizard dialog box opens, in which you choose names for the main form and the subform.

   You will use Customer Orders as the main form name and Order Subform as the subform name.

4. Position the insertion point to the right of the last letter in the Form text box, press the **spacebar**, and then type **Orders**. The main form name is now Customer Orders. Note that the default subform name, Order Subform, is the name you want, so you don't need to change it.

   You have answered all the Form Wizard questions.

5. Click the **Finish** button. After a few moments, the completed form is displayed in Form view.

   Depending on your monitor's resolution, one or more of the columns in the subform might not be wide enough to display the field names entirely. If so, you need to resize the columns to their best fit.

6. Double-click the pointer ✛ at the right edge of each column in the subform. The columns are resized to their best fit and all field names are fully displayed. See Figure 4-16.

| Figure 4-16 | COMPLETED FORM |

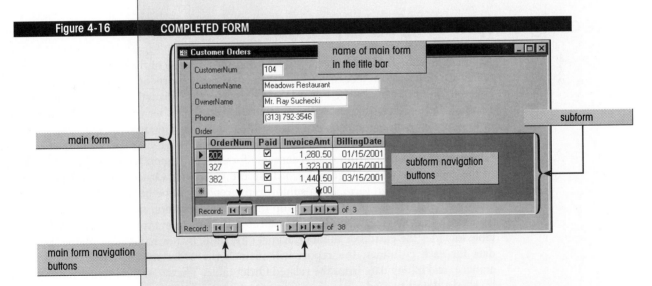

In the main form, Access displays the fields from the first record in the Customer table in columnar format. The records in the main form appear in primary key sequence by customer number. Customer 104 has three related records in the Order table; these records are shown in the subform in a datasheet format. The form shows that Meadows Restaurant has placed three orders with Valle Coffee, and each order has been paid.

Two sets of navigation buttons appear near the bottom of the form. You use the top set of navigation buttons to select records from the related table in the subform, and the bottom set to select records from the primary table in the main form.

You'll use the navigation buttons to view different records.

To navigate to different main form and subform records:

1. Click the **Last Record** navigation button ▶︎❙ in the main form. Record 38 in the Customer table for Embers Restaurant becomes the current record in the main form. The subform shows that this customer has placed three orders with Valle Coffee, all of which are unpaid.

2. Click the **Last Record** navigation button ▶︎❙ in the subform. Record 3 in the Order table becomes the current record in the subform.

3. Click the **Previous Record** navigation button ◀︎ in the main form. Record 37 in the Customer table for The Empire becomes the current record in the main form. This customer has placed two orders, both of which are unpaid.

   You have finished your work with the form, so you can close it.

4. Click the **Close** button ✕ on the form title bar. The form closes, and you return to the Database window. Notice that both the main form, Customer Orders, and the subform, Order Subform, appear in the Forms list box.

Kim would like a report showing data from both the Customer and Order tables so that all the pertinent information about restaurant customers and their orders is available in one place.

Creating a Report Using the Report Wizard

As you learned in Tutorial 1, a report is a formatted hardcopy of the contents of one or more tables in a database. In Access, you can create your own reports or use the Report Wizard to create them for you. Like the Form Wizard, the **Report Wizard** asks you a series of questions and then creates a report based on your answers. Whether you use the Report Wizard or design your own report, you can change the report's design after you create it.

Kim wants you to create a report that includes selected customer data from the Customer table and all the orders from the Order table for each customer. Kim has sketched a design of the report she wants (Figure 4-17). Like the Customer Orders form you just created, which includes a main form and a subform, the report will be based on both tables, which are joined in a one-to-many relationship through the common field of CustomerNum. As shown in the sketch in Figure 4-17, the selected customer data from the primary Customer table includes the customer number, name, city, state, owner name, and phone. Below the data for each customer, the report will include the order number, paid status, invoice amount, and billing date from the related Order table. The set of field values for each order is called a **detail record**.

Figure 4-17   **REPORT SKETCH FOR THE CUSTOMERS AND ORDERS REPORT**

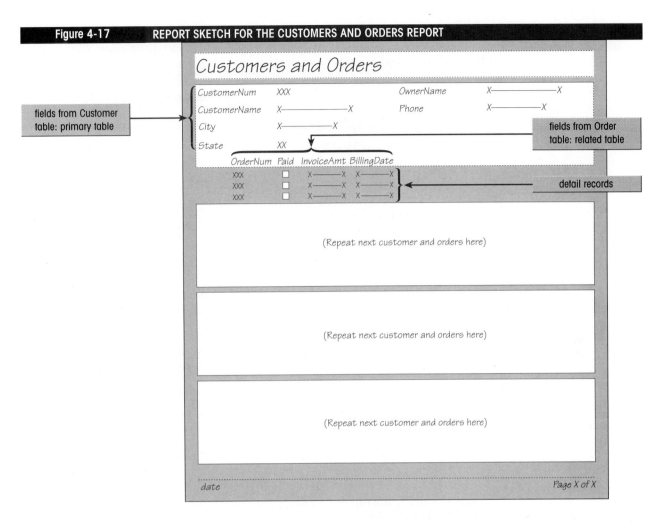

You'll use the Report Wizard to create the report according to the design in Kim's sketch.

To start the Report Wizard and select the fields to include in the report:

1. Click **Reports** in the Objects bar of the Database window to display the Reports list box. You have not yet created and saved any reports.

2. Click the **New** button in the Database window. The New Report dialog box opens.

   Although the data for the report exists in two tables (Customer and Order), you can choose only one table or query to be the data source for the report in the New Report dialog box. However, in the Report Wizard dialog boxes you can include data from other tables. You will select the primary Customer table in the New Report dialog box.

3. Click **Report Wizard**, click the list arrow for choosing a table or query, and then click **Customer**. See Figure 4-18.

| Figure 4-18 | COMPLETED NEW REPORT DIALOG BOX |

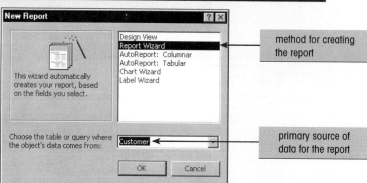

method for creating
the report

primary source of
data for the report

4. Click the **OK** button. The first Report Wizard dialog box opens.

In the first Report Wizard dialog box, you select fields in the order you want them to appear on the report. Kim wants the CustomerNum, CustomerName, City, State, OwnerName, and Phone fields from the Customer table to appear on the report.

5. Click **CustomerNum** in the Available Fields list box (if necessary), and then click the ▷ button. The field moves to the Selected Fields list box.

6. Repeat Step 5 for **CustomerName**, **City**, **State**, **OwnerName**, and **Phone**.

7. Click the **Tables/Queries** list arrow, and then click **Table: Order**. The fields from the Order table appear in the Available Fields list box.

The CustomerNum field will appear on the report with the customer data, so you do not have to include it in the detail records for each order. Otherwise, Kim wants all the fields from the Order table to be included in the report. The easiest way to include the necessary fields is to add all the Order table fields to the Selected Fields list box, and then to remove the only field you don't want to include—CustomerNum.

8. Click the ▷▷ button to move all the fields from the Available Fields list box to the Selected Fields list box.

9. Click **Order.CustomerNum** in the Selected Fields list box, click the ◁ button to move the selected field back to the Available Fields list box, and then click the **Next** button. The second Report Wizard dialog box opens. See Figure 4-19.

Figure 4-19   CHOOSING A GROUPED OR UNGROUPED REPORT

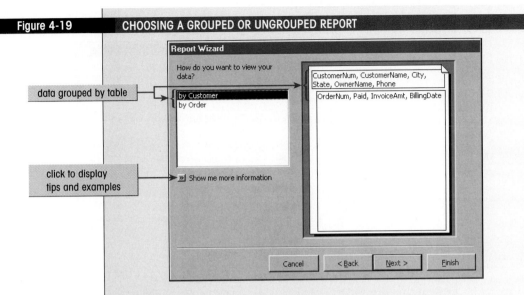

data grouped by table

click to display
tips and examples

You can choose to arrange the selected data grouped by table, which is the default, or ungrouped. For a grouped report, the data from a record in the primary table appears as a group, followed by the joined records from the related table. For the report you are creating, data from a record in the Customer table appears in a group, followed by the records for the customer from the Order table. An example of an ungrouped report would be a report of records from the Customer and Order tables in order by OrderNum. Each order and its associated customer data would appear together; the data would not be grouped by table.

You can display tips and examples for the choices in the Report Wizard dialog box by clicking the "Show me more information" button [»].

To display tips about the options in the Report Wizard dialog box:

1. Click the [»] button. The Report Wizard Tips dialog box opens. Read the displayed information in the dialog box.

   You can display examples of different grouping methods by clicking the [»] button ("Show me examples").

2. Click the [»] button. The Report Wizard Examples dialog box opens. See Figure 4-20.

Figure 4-20	REPORT WIZARD EXAMPLES DIALOG BOX

click to display examples

click to return to Report
Wizard Tips dialog box

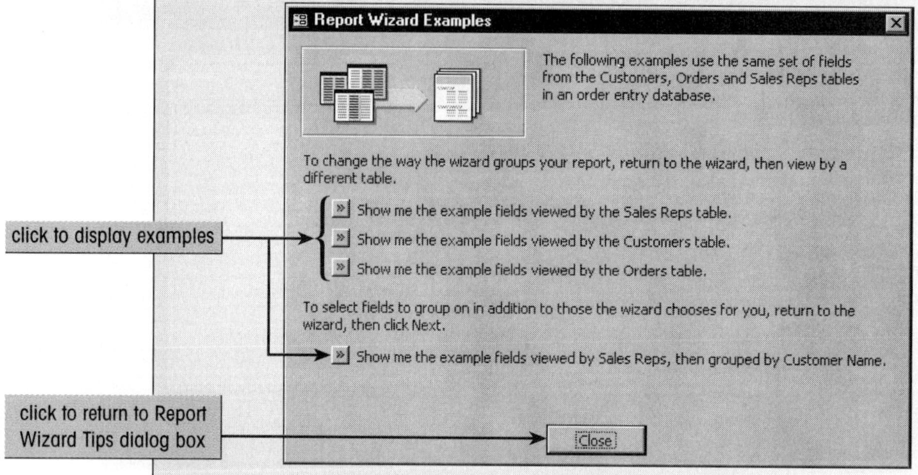

You can display examples of different grouping methods by clicking the ⟫ buttons.

3. Click each ⟫ button in turn, review the displayed example, and then click the **Close** button to return to the Report Wizard Examples dialog box.

4. Click the **Close** button to return to the Report Wizard Tips dialog box, and then click the **Close** button to return to the second Report Wizard dialog box.

The default options shown on your screen are correct for the report Kim wants, so you can continue responding to the Report Wizard questions.

To finish creating the report using the Report Wizard:

1. Click the **Next** button. The next Report Wizard dialog box opens, in which you choose additional grouping levels.

   Two grouping levels are shown: one for a customer's data, and the other for a customer's orders. Grouping levels are useful for reports with multiple levels, such as those containing monthly, quarterly, and annual totals, or those containing city and country groups. Kim's report contains no further grouping levels, so you can accept the default options.

2. Click the **Next** button. The next Report Wizard dialog box opens, in which you choose the sort order for the detail records. See Figure 4-21.

Figure 4-21   CHOOSING THE SORT ORDER FOR DETAIL RECORDS

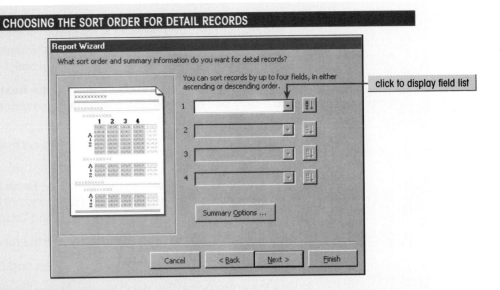

click to display field list

The records from the Order table for a customer represent the detail records for Kim's report. She wants these records to appear in increasing, or ascending, order by the value in the OrderNum field.

3. Click the **1** list arrow, click **OrderNum**, and then click the **Next** button. The next Report Wizard dialog box opens, in which you choose a layout and page orientation for the report. See Figure 4-22.

Figure 4-22   CHOOSING THE REPORT LAYOUT AND PAGE ORIENTATION

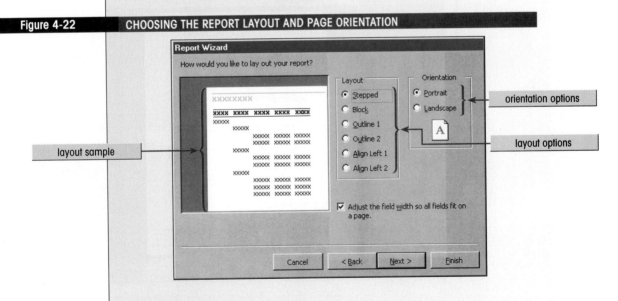

layout sample

orientation options

layout options

A sample of each layout appears in the box on the left.

4. Click each layout option and examine each sample that appears. You'll use the Outline 2 layout option because it resembles the layout shown in Kim's sketch of the report.

5. Click the **Outline 2** option button, and then click the **Next** button. The next Report Wizard dialog box opens, in which you choose a style for the report.

A sample of the selected style, or AutoFormat, appears in the box on the left. You can always choose a different AutoFormat after you create the report, just as you can when creating a form. Kim likes the appearance of the Corporate AutoFormat, so you'll choose this one for your report.

6. Click **Corporate** (if necessary) and then click the **Next** button. The last Report Wizard dialog box opens, in which you choose a report name, which also serves as the printed title on the report.

According to Kim's sketch, the report title you need to specify is "Customers and Orders."

7. Type **Customers and Orders** and then click the **Finish** button. The Report Wizard creates the report based on your answers and saves it as an object in your database. Then Access opens the Customers and Orders report in Print Preview.

To view the report better, you need to maximize the report window.

8. Click the **Maximize** button 🔲 on the Customers and Orders title bar.

To view the entire page, you need to change the Zoom setting.

9. Click the **Zoom** list arrow on the Print Preview toolbar, and then click **Fit**. The first page of the report is displayed in Print Preview. See Figure 4-23.

Figure 4-23	REPORT DISPLAYED IN PRINT PREVIEW

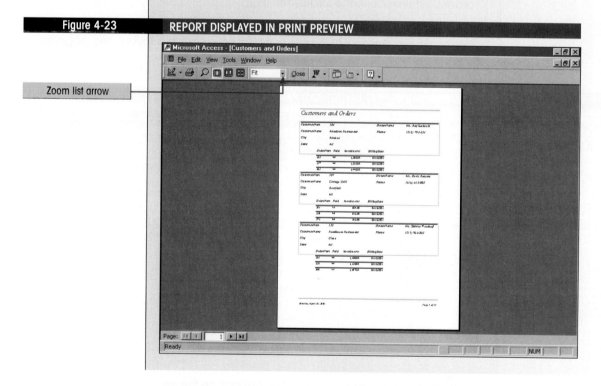

Zoom list arrow

When a report is displayed in Print Preview, you can use the pointer to toggle between a full-page display and a close-up display of the report. Kim asks you to check the report to see if any adjustments need to be made. To do so, you need to view a close-up display of the report.

To view a close-up display of the report and make any necessary corrections:

1. Click the pointer ⊕ at the top center of the report. The display changes to show the report close up. See Figure 4-24. The last digit in each phone number might not be visible in the report on your screen. To fix this, you first need to display the report in Design view.

Figure 4-24   **CLOSE-UP VIEW OF THE REPORT**

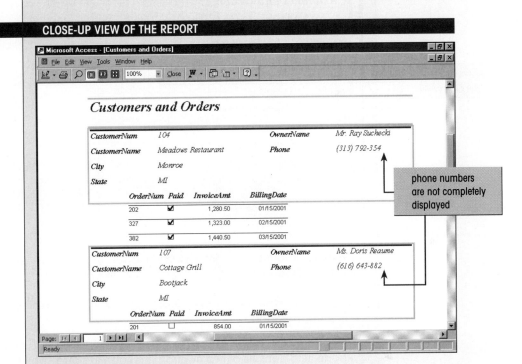

TROUBLE? Scroll your screen as necessary so that it matches the screen in Figure 4-24.

TROUBLE? If the phone numbers on your report are displayed correctly, follow the remaining steps so you will know how to make corrections, even though you will not need to resize the field.

2. Click the **View** button for Design view ⊠ on the Print Preview toolbar. Access displays the report in Design view. See Figure 4-25.

| Figure 4-25 | REPORT DISPLAYED IN DESIGN VIEW |

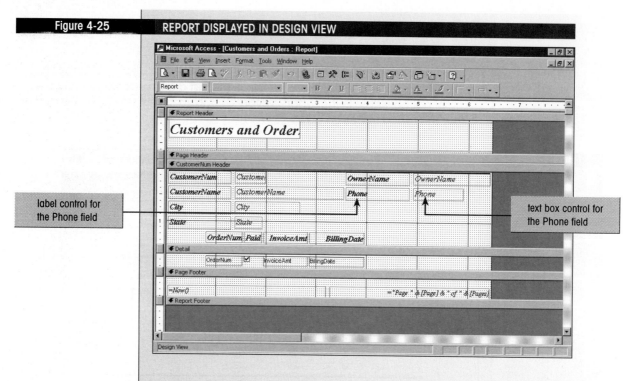

label control for
the Phone field

text box control for
the Phone field

TROUBLE? If your screen displays any window other than those shown in Figure 4-25, click the Close button ☒ on the window's title bar to close it.

You use the Report window in Design view to modify existing reports and to create custom reports.

Each item on a report in Design view is called a **control**. For example, the Phone field consists of two controls: the label "Phone," which appears on the report to identify the field value, and the Phone text box, in which the actual field value appears. You need to widen the text box control for the Phone field so that the entire field value is visible in the report.

3. Click the text box control for the Phone field to select it. Notice that small black boxes appear on the border around the control. These boxes, which are called **handles**, indicate that the control is selected and can be manipulated.

4. Position the pointer on the center right handle of the Phone text box control until the pointer changes to ↔. See Figure 4-26.

Figure 4-26	RESIZING THE PHONE TEXT BOX CONTROL

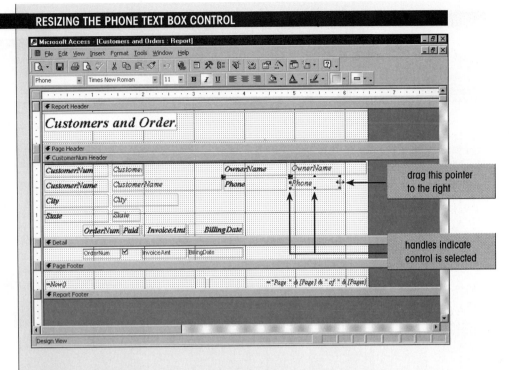

5. Click and drag the pointer to the right until the right edge of the control is aligned with the 6-inch mark on the horizontal ruler, and then release the mouse button.

Now you need to switch back to Print Preview and make sure that the complete value for the Phone field is visible.

6. Click the **View** button for Print Preview 🔍 on the Report Design toolbar. The report appears in Print Preview. Notice that the Phone field values are now completely displayed.

7. Click **File** on the menu bar, and then click **Save** to save the modified report.

Kim decides that she wants the report to include the Valle Coffee cup logo to the right of the report title, for visual interest. You can add the logo to the report by inserting a picture of the coffee cup.

Inserting a Picture in a Report

In Access, you can insert a picture or other graphic image in a report or form to enhance the appearance of the report or form. Sources of graphic images include Microsoft Paint, other drawing programs, and scanners. The file containing the picture you need to insert is named VallCup, and is located in the Tutorial folder on your Data Disk.

To insert the picture in the report:

1. Click the **Close** button on the Print Preview toolbar to display the report in Design view. See Figure 4-27.

Figure 4-27   INSERTING A PICTURE IN DESIGN VIEW

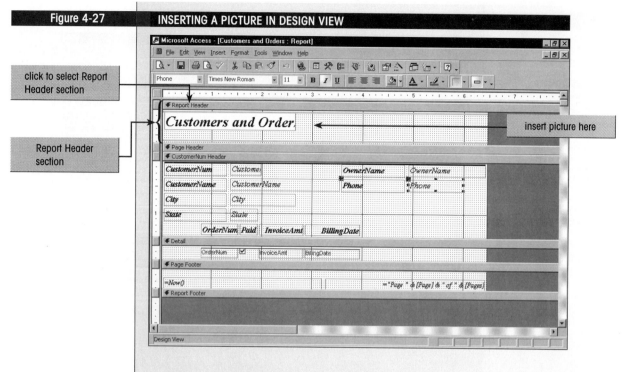

Kim wants the picture to appear on the first page of the report only; therefore, you need to insert the picture in the Report Header section (see Figure 4-27). Any text or graphics placed in this section appear once at the beginning of the report.

2. Click the **Report Header** bar to select this section of the report. The bar is highlighted to indicate that the section is selected.

3. Click **Insert** on the menu bar, and then click **Picture**. The Insert Picture dialog box opens. See Figure 4-28.

Figure 4-28   INSERT PICTURE DIALOG BOX

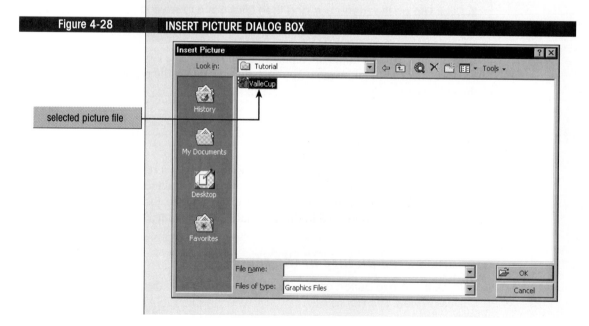

4. If necessary, open the Tutorial folder on your Data Disk, click **ValleCup** to select the picture of the Valle Coffee cup, and then click the **OK** button. The picture is inserted at the far left of the Report Header section, covering some of the report title text. See Figure 4-29.

Figure 4-29	PICTURE INSERTED IN REPORT

top border line of report

inserted picture

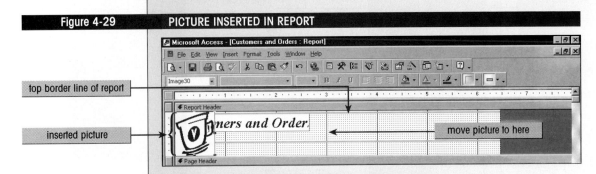

Notice that handles appear on the border around the picture, indicating that the picture is selected and can be manipulated.

Kim wants the picture to appear to the right of the report title, so you need to move the picture using the mouse.

5. Position the pointer on the picture until the pointer changes to 🖐, and then click and drag the mouse to move the picture to the right so that its left edge aligns with the 3-inch mark on the horizontal ruler and its top edge is just below the top border line above the report title (see Figure 4-29).

6. Release the mouse button. The picture appears in the new position. See Figure 4-30.

Figure 4-30	REPOSITIONED PICTURE IN THE REPORT

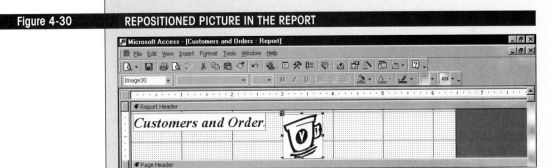

TROUBLE? If your picture is in a different location from the one shown in Figure 4-30, use the pointer 🖐 to reposition the picture until it is in approximately the same position shown in the figure. Be sure that the top edge of the picture is below the top border line of the report.

7. Click the **View** button for Print Preview 🔍 on the Report Design toolbar to view the report in Print Preview. The report now includes the inserted picture. If necessary, click the **Zoom** button 🔍 on the Print Preview toolbar to display the entire report page. See Figure 4-31.

| Figure 4-31 | PRINT PREVIEW OF REPORT WITH PICTURE |

picture included
in report

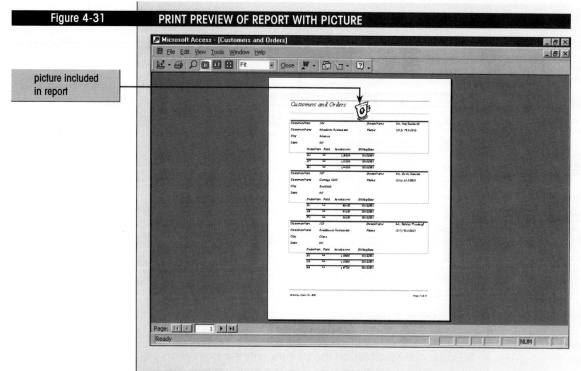

8. Click **File** on the menu bar, and then click **Save** to save the changes you made to the report.

The report is now complete. You'll print a hardcopy of just the first page of the report so that Kim can review the report layout and the inserted picture.

To print page 1 of the report:

1. Click **File** on the menu bar, and then click **Print**. The Print dialog box opens.

2. In the Print Range section, click the **Pages** option button. The insertion point now appears in the From text box so that you can specify the range of pages to print.

3. Type **1** in the From text box, press the **Tab** key to move to the To text box, and then type **1**. These settings specify that only page 1 of the report will be printed.

4. Click the **OK** button. The Print dialog box closes, and the first page of the report is printed. See Figure 4-32.

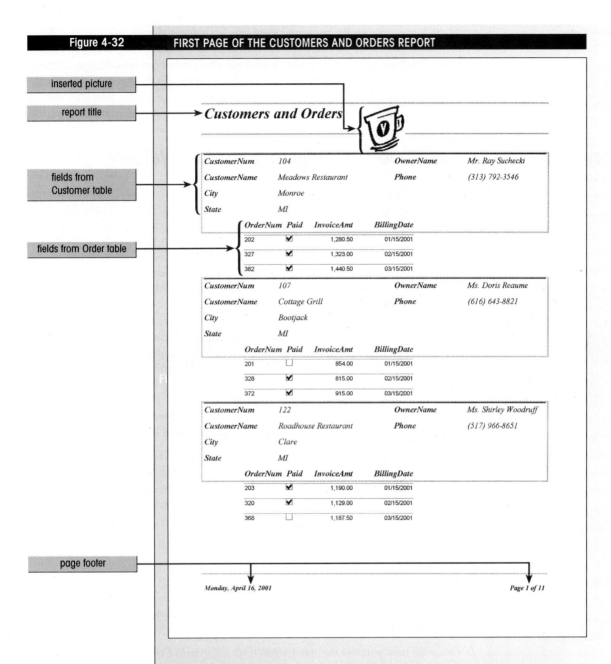

Figure 4-32   **FIRST PAGE OF THE CUSTOMERS AND ORDERS REPORT**

inserted picture

report title

Customers and Orders

fields from
Customer table

CustomerNum	104	OwnerName	Mr. Ray Suchecki
CustomerName	Meadows Restaurant	Phone	(313) 792-3546
City	Monroe		
State	MI		

OrderNum	Paid	InvoiceAmt	BillingDate
202	✔	1,280.50	01/15/2001
327	✔	1,323.00	02/15/2001
382	✔	1,440.50	03/15/2001

fields from Order table

CustomerNum	107	OwnerName	Ms. Doris Reaume
CustomerName	Cottage Grill	Phone	(616) 643-8821
City	Bootjack		
State	MI		

OrderNum	Paid	InvoiceAmt	BillingDate
201	☐	854.00	01/15/2001
328	✔	815.00	02/15/2001
372	✔	915.00	03/15/2001

CustomerNum	122	OwnerName	Ms. Shirley Woodruff
CustomerName	Roadhouse Restaurant	Phone	(517) 966-8651
City	Clare		
State	MI		

OrderNum	Paid	InvoiceAmt	BillingDate
203	✔	1,190.00	01/15/2001
320	✔	1,129.00	02/15/2001
368	☐	1,187.50	03/15/2001

page footer

Monday, April 16, 2001   *Page 1 of 11*

TROUBLE? Depending on the printer you're using, the total number of pages in your report might be fewer or greater than the total indicated in the figure.

Kim approves of the report layout and contents, so you can close the report.

5. Click the **Close** button ☒ on the menu bar.

TROUBLE? If you click the Close button on the Print Preview toolbar by mistake, Access redisplays the report in Design view. Click the Close button ☒ on the menu bar.

6. Click the **Close** button ☒ on the Access title bar to close the database and exit Access.

Kim shows her report to Barbara, and they are both pleased with the results. However, Barbara wants to consider the fact that Valle Coffee is in the process of upgrading all of its users to have Access 2000 on their computers—employees who do not yet have Access 2000 might not be able to contribute their suggestions and feedback on the development of the Restaurant database. Barbara asks Kim to consider converting the database to the previous version of Access, so that all employees can inspect and use the database during the conversion period.

Converting an Access 2000 Database to a Previous Version

Access 2000 includes a new feature that lets you convert a database to the previous version, Access 97. When you convert an Access 2000 database to Access 97 format, any functionality that is specific to Access 2000 is lost. However, the database's structure and data will be useable in the converted database. To convert a database, open it in the Database window, click Tools on the menu bar, point to Database Utilities, point to Convert Database, and then click To Prior Access Database Version. The Convert Database Into dialog box will open, in which you can specify a filename and location for the converted database. After you click the Save button, Access 2000 will convert the database and save it as an Access 97 database, so that Access 97 users will be able to open the database as if it were created in Access 97.

If you try to open an Access 97 database in Access 2000, the Convert/Open Database dialog box will open and offer you two options: convert the database to Access 2000 format, or open the database in Access 97 format. When you are sharing a database with Access 97 users, you should select the "open" option so the database will be usable with both Access versions. Kim and Barbara might decide to convert and use the Restaurant database in Access 97 format while all database users are being upgraded to Access 2000. When every employee has Access 2000, the database can be opened and used in Access 2000 format only.

Barbara is satisfied that the forms you created—the Order Data form and the Customer Orders form—will make it easier to enter, view, and update data in the Restaurant database. The Customers and Orders report presents important information about Valle Coffee's restaurant customers in an attractive and professional format, which will help Kim and her staff in their sales and marketing efforts.

Session 4.2 QUICK CHECK

1. How are a related table and a primary table associated with a form that contains a main form and a subform?

2. Describe how you use the navigation buttons to move through a form containing a main form and a subform.

3. When you use the Report Wizard, the report name is also used as the _____ .

4. Each item on a report in Design view is called a(n) _____ .

5. To insert a picture in a report, the report must be displayed in _____ .

6. Any text or graphics placed in the _____ section of a report will appear only on the first page of the report.

7. Describe one advantage and one disadvantage of converting an Access 2000 database to Access 97 format.

REVIEW ASSIGNMENTS

Barbara wants to enhance the **Valle Products** database with forms and reports, and she asks you to complete the following:

1. Make sure your Data Disk is in the disk drive, start Access, and then open the **Valle Products** database located in the Review folder on your Data Disk.

2. Use the Form Wizard to create a form based on the **Product** table. Select all fields for the form, the Columnar layout, the SandStone style, and the title **Product Data** for the form.

3. Using the form you created in the previous step, print the fifth form record, change the AutoFormat to Sumi Painting, save the changed form, and then print the fifth form record again.

4. Use the **Product Data** form to update the **Product** table as follows:
   a. Navigate to the record with the ProductCode 2410. Change the field values for WeightCode to A, Decaf to D, and Price to 8.99 for this record.
   b. Use the Find command to move to the record with the ProductCode 4306, and then delete the record.
   c. Add a new record with the following field values:

   ProductCode: 2306
   CoffeeCode: AMAR
   WeightCode: A
   Decaf: Null
   Price: 7.99

   d. Print only this form record, and then save and close the form.

Explore 5. Use the AutoForm: Columnar Wizard to create a form based on the **New Prices** query. Save the form as **New Prices**, and then close the form.

6. Use the Form Wizard to create a form containing a main form and a subform. Select the CoffeeName and CoffeeType fields from the **Coffee** table for the main form, and select all fields except CoffeeCode from the **Product** table for the subform. Use the Datasheet layout and the Sumi Painting style. Specify the title **Coffee Products** for the main form and the title **Product Subform** for the subform. Resize all columns in the subform to their best fit. Print the eighth main form record and its subform records. Close the form.

Explore 7. Use the Report Wizard to create a report based on the primary **Coffee** table and the related **Product** table. Select all fields from the **Coffee** table except Decaf, and select all fields from the **Product** table except CoffeeCode. In the third Report Wizard dialog box, specify the CoffeeType field as an additional grouping level. Sort the detail records by ProductCode. Choose the Align Left 2 layout and the Formal style for the report. Specify the title **Valle Coffee Products** for the report.

8. Insert the ValleCup picture, which is located in the Review folder on your Data Disk, in the Report Header section of the **Valle Coffee Products** report. Position the picture so that its left edge aligns with the 4-inch mark on the horizontal ruler and its top edge is just below the top border line of the report.

9. Print only the first page of the report, and then close and save the modified report.

10. Close the **Valle Products** database, and then exit Access.

CASE PROBLEMS

Case 1. Ashbrook Mall Information Desk   Sam Bullard wants the **MallJobs** database to include forms and reports that will help him track and distribute information about jobs available at the Ashbrook Mall. You'll create the necessary forms and reports by completing the following:

1. Make sure your Data Disk is in the disk drive, start Access, and then open the **MallJobs** database located in the Cases folder on your Data Disk.

2. Use the Form Wizard to create a form based on the **Store** table. Select all fields for the form, the Columnar layout, and the Blends style. Specify the title **Store Data** for the form.

3. Change the AutoFormat for the **Store Data** form to Standard.

4. Use the Find command to move to the record with the Store value of TH, and then change the Contact field value for this record to Sarah Pedicini.

5. Use the **Store Data** form to add a new record with the following field values:
   Store: PW
   StoreName: Pet World
   Location: B2
   Contact: Ryan Shevlin
   Extension: 2311

   Print only this form record, and then save and close the form.

6. Use the Form Wizard to create a form containing a main form and a subform. Select all the fields from the **Store** table for the main form, and select all fields except Store from the **Job** table for the subform. Use the Tabular layout and the Standard style. Specify the title **Jobs By Store** for the main form and the title **Job Subform** for the subform.

7. Print the ninth main form record and its subform records, and then close the **Jobs By Store** form.

8. Use the Report Wizard to create a report based on the primary **Store** table and the related **Job** table. Select all the fields from the **Store** table, and select all the fields from the **Job** table except Store. Sort the detail records by Job. Choose the Align Left 2 layout and Landscape orientation for the report. Choose the Casual style. Specify the title **Available Jobs** for the report, and then print and close the report.

9. Close the **MallJobs** database, and then exit Access.

Case 2. Professional Litigation User Services   Raj Jawahir continues his work with the **Payments** database to track and analyze the payment history of PLUS clients. To help him, you'll enhance the **Payments** database by completing the following:

1. Make sure your Data Disk is in the disk drive, start Access, and then open the **Payments** database located in the Cases folder on your Data Disk.

2. Use the Form Wizard to create a form containing a main form and a subform. Select the Firm# and FirmName fields from the **Firm** table for the main form, and select all fields except Firm# from the **Payment** table for the subform. Use the Datasheet layout and the Industrial style. Specify the title **Firm Payments** for the main form and the title **Payment Subform** for the subform. Resize all columns in the subform to their best fit. Print the first main form record and its displayed subform records.

3. For the form you just created, change the AutoFormat to SandStone, save the changed form, and then print the first main form record and its displayed subform records.

4. Navigate to the second record in the subform for the first main record, and then change the AmtPaid field value to 1,800.00.

5. Use the Find command to move to the record with the Firm# 1142, and delete the record. Answer Yes to any warning messages about deleting the record.

Explore   6. Use the appropriate wildcard character to find all records with the abbreviation "DA" (for District Attorney) anywhere in the firm name. (*Hint*: You must enter the wildcard character before and after the text you are searching for.) How many records did you find? Close the **Firm Payments** form.

Explore   7. Use the Report Wizard to create a report based on the primary **Firm** table and the related **Payment** table. Select all fields from the **Firm** table except Extension, and select all fields from the **Payment** table except Firm#. In the third Report Wizard dialog box, specify the PLUSAcctRep field as an additional grouping level. Sort the detail records by AmtPaid in *descending* order. Choose the Block layout, Landscape orientation, and the Bold style for the report. Specify the title **Payments By Firms** for the report.

8. Insert the PLUS picture, which is located in the Cases folder on your Data Disk, in the Report Header section of the **Payments By Firms** report. Leave the picture in its original position at the left edge of the report header.

Explore   9. Use the Office Assistant to ask the following question: "How do I move an object behind another?" Click the topic "Move a text box or other control in front of or behind other controls." Read the information and then close the Help window. Make sure the PLUS picture is still selected, and then move it behind the Payments By Firms title.

Explore   10. Use the Office Assistant to ask the following question: "How do I change the background color of an object?" Click the topic "Change the background color of a control or section." Read the information and then close the Help window and hide the Office Assistant. Select the Payments By Firms title object, and then change its background color to Transparent.

11. Display the report in Print Preview. Print just the first page of the report, and then close and save the report.

12. Close the **Payments** database, and then exit Access.

Case 3. Best Friends   Noah and Sheila Warnick want to create forms and reports for the **Walks** database. You'll help them create these database objects by completing the following:

1. Make sure your Data Disk is in the disk drive, start Access, and then open the **Walks** database located in the Cases folder on your Data Disk.

2. Use the Form Wizard to create a form based on the **Walker** table. Select all fields for the form, the Columnar layout, and the Blueprint style. Specify the title **Walker Data** for the form.

3. Use the **Walker Data** form to update the **Walker** table as follows:

   a. For the record with the WalkerID 175, change the LastName to Petr and the Distance to 2.0.

   b. Add a new record with the following values:
      WalkerID: 225
      LastName: Bethel
      FirstName: Martha
      Phone: 711-0825
      Distance: 2.7

   c. Print just this form record.

   d. Delete the record with the WalkerID field value of 187.

4. Change the AutoFormat of the **Walker Data** form to Expedition, save the changed form, and then use the form to print the last record in the **Walker** table. Close the form.

5. Use the Form Wizard to create a form containing a main form and a subform. Select all the fields from the **Walker** table for the main form, and select the Pledger, PledgeAmt, PaidAmt, and DatePaid fields from the **Pledge** table for the subform. Use the Tabular layout and the Expedition style. Specify the title **Walkers And Pledges** for the main form and the title **Pledge Subform** for the subform. Close the form.

Explore 6. Open the **Pledge Subform** in Design view. In the Form Header section, reduce the width of the PledgeAmt, PaidAmt, and DatePaid controls so that the control boxes are just slightly wider than the field names. (*Hint*: Select each control and use the pointer ↔ on the middle right handle to resize each control.) Repeat this procedure to resize the same controls in the Detail section of the form. Then, use the pointer ✋ to move these same controls—in both the Form Header section and the Detail section—to the left, so that the right edge of the DatePaid control (in each section) aligns approximately with the 3½-inch mark on the horizontal ruler. Close and save the **Pledge Subform**. Then, open the **Walkers And Pledges** form in Form view. Use the navigation buttons to find the first main form record that contains values in the subform. If any field values in the subform are not fully visible because of the resizing, close the **Walkers And Pledges** form, open the **Pledge Subform** in Design view, and make any necessary adjustments so that all four fields in the subform appear in the **Walkers And Pledges** form, and so that all field values are fully visible in the subform. Then reopen the form and display the first main form record with values in the subform.

7. Print the current main form record and its subform records, and then close the **Walkers And Pledges** form.

8. Use the Report Wizard to create a report based on the primary **Walker** table and the related **Pledge** table. Select all fields from the **Walker** table, and select all fields from the **Pledge** table except WalkerID. Sort the detail records by PledgeNo. Choose the Align Left 2 layout and Landscape orientation for the report. Choose the Formal style. Specify the title **Walk-A-Thon Walkers And Pledges** for the report.

Explore 9. View both pages of the report in Print Preview. (*Hint*: Use a toolbar button.) Print the entire report, and then close it.

10. Close the **Walks** database, and then exit Access.

Case 4. Lopez Lexus Dealerships   Maria and Hector Lopez want to create forms and reports that will help them track and analyze data about the cars and different locations for their Lexus dealerships. Help them enhance the **Lexus** database by completing the following:

1. Make sure your Data Disk is in the disk drive, start Access, and then open the **Lexus** database located in the Cases folder on your Data Disk.

2. Use the Form Wizard to create a form containing a main form and a subform. Select all the fields from the **Locations** table for the main form, and select the VehicleID, Model, Class, Year, Cost, and SellingPrice fields from the **Cars** table for the subform. Use the Datasheet layout and the Standard style. Specify the title **Locations And Cars** for the main form and the title **Cars Subform** for the subform. Resize all columns in the sub-form to their best fit. Print the first main form record and its displayed subform records.

3. For the form you just created, change the AutoFormat to International, save the changed form, and then print the first main form record and its displayed subform records.

4. Navigate to the third record in the subform for the seventh main record, and then change the SellingPrice field value to $49,875.00.

5. Use the Find command to move to the record with the LocationCode P1, and delete the record. Answer Yes to any warning messages about deleting the record.

6. Use the appropriate wildcard character to find all records with a LocationCode value that begins with the letter "H." How many records did you find? Close the form.

Explore ▶ 7. Use the Report Wizard to create a report based on the primary **Locations** table and the related **Cars** table. Select all fields from the **Locations** table, and select all fields from the **Cars** table except Manufacturer, Transmission, and LocationCode. Specify two sort fields for the detail records: first, the Year field in ascending order, then the SellingPrice field in descending order. Choose the Outline 1 layout and Landscape orientation for the report. Choose the Compact style. Specify the title **Dealership Locations And Cars** for the report.

Explore ▶ 8. View the first two pages of the report in Print Preview at the same time. (*Hint*: Use a toolbar button.) Print the first two report pages, and then close the report.

9. Close the **Lexus** database, and then exit Access.

INTERNET ASSIGNMENTS

The purpose of the Internet Assignments is to challenge you to find information on the Internet that you can use to create effective documents. The actual assignments are updated and maintained on the Course Technology Web site. Log on to the Internet and use your Web browser to go to the Student Online Companion to accompany this text at **www.course.com/NewPerspectives/office2000**. Click the Access link, and then click the link for Tutorial 4.

QUICK CHECK ANSWERS

Session 4.1

1. The AutoForm Wizard creates a form automatically using all the fields in the selected table or query; the Form Wizard allows you to choose some or all of the fields in the selected table or query, choose fields from other tables and queries, and display fields in any order on the form.

2. An AutoFormat is a predefined style for a form (or report). To change a form's AutoFormat, display the form in Design view, click the AutoFormat button on the Form Design toolbar, click the new AutoFormat in the Form AutoFormats list box, and then click the OK button.

3. the last record in the table

4. datasheet

5. the question mark (?)

6. as many form records as can fit on a printed page

Session 4.2

1. The main form displays the data from the primary table, and the subform displays the data from the related table.

2. You use the top set of navigation buttons to select and move through records from the related table in the subform, and the bottom set to select and move through records from the primary table in the main form.

3. report title

4. control

5. Design view

6. Report Header

7. One advantage is that users of the database who do not have Access 2000 can inspect and use the converted database; a disadvantage is that the converted database will not include functionality that is specific to Access 2000.

TASK	PAGE #	RECOMMENDED METHOD
Access, exit	AC 1.13	Click ⊠ on the program window
Access, start	AC 1.07	Click Start, point to Programs, click Microsoft Access
Aggregate functions, use	AC 3.34	Display the query in Design view, click Σ
AutoForm, create	AC 4.02	Click Forms in the Objects bar, click New, click an AutoForm Wizard, choose the table or query for the form, click OK
AutoFormat, change	AC 4.05	See Reference Window: Changing a Form's AutoFormat
AutoReport, create	AC 4.19	Click Reports in the Objects bar, click New, click an AutoReport Wizard, choose the table or query for the form, click OK
Calculated field, add to a query	AC 3.31	See Reference Window: Using Expression Builder
Column, adjust width of	AC 3.23	Double-click the right border of the column heading
Data, find	AC 4.08	See Reference Window: Finding Data
Database, compact and repair	AC 1.25	Click Tools on the menu bar, point to Database Utilities, click Compact and Repair Database
Database, compact on close	AC 1.26	Click Tools on the menu bar, click Options, click the General tab, click Compact on Close, click OK
Datasheet view, switch to	AC 2.17	Click ▦
Design view, switch to	AC 2.22	Click ◩
Field, add	AC 2.23	See Reference Window: Adding a Field Between Two Existing Fields
Field, define	AC 2.08	See Reference Window: Defining a Field in a Table
Field, delete	AC 2.21	Display the table in Design view, right-click the field's row selector, click Delete Rows
Field, move	AC 2.22	Display the table in Design view, click the field's row selector, drag the field with the pointer
Filter By Selection, activate	AC 3.18	See Reference Window: Using Filter By Selection
Form Wizard, activate	AC 4.02	Click Forms in the Objects bar, click New, click Form Wizard, choose the table or query for the form, click OK
Office Assistant, use to get Help	AC 1.20	See Reference Window: Using the Office Assistant
Picture, insert on a report	AC 4.27	Click Insert on the menu bar, click Picture, select the picture file, click OK
Primary key, specify	AC 2.15	See Reference Window: Specifying a Primary Key for a Table
Query, define	AC 3.03	Click Queries in the Objects bar, click New, click Design View, click OK
Query, run	AC 3.05	Click ❗

TASK	PAGE #	RECOMMENDED METHOD
Query results, sort	AC 3.15	See Reference Window: Sorting a Query Datasheet
Record, add a new one	AC 2.17	Click ▶＊
Record, delete	AC 2.30	Right-click the record's row selector, click Delete Record, click Yes
Record, move to first	AC 1.12	Click ◄◄
Record, move to last	AC 1.12	Click ▶▶
Record, move to next	AC 1.12	Click ▶
Record, move to previous	AC 1.12	Click ◄
Record, move to a specific one	AC 1.12	Type the record number in the Specific Record box, press Enter
Records, redisplay all after filter	AC 3.19	Click ▽
Relationship, define between two tables	AC 3.08	Click ⊟
Report Wizard, activate	AC 4.19	Click Reports in the Objects bar, click New, click Report Wizard, choose the table or query for the report, click OK
Sort, specify ascending	AC 3.13	Click ᴬ↓
Sort, specify descending	AC 3.13	Click ᶻ↓
Table, create	AC 2.07	Click Tables in the Objects bar, click New, click Design View, click OK
Table, open	AC 1.11	Click Tables in the Objects bar, click the table name, click Open
Table, print	AC 1.13	Click 🖨
Table structure, save	AC 2.16	See Reference Window: Saving a Table Structure

File Finder

Location in Tutorial	Name and Location of Data File	Student Creates New File
ACCESS LEVEL 1		
Tutorial 1		
Session 1.1	Disk1\Tutorial\Restaurant.mdb	
Session 1.2	Disk1\Tutorial\Restaurant.mdb	
Review Assignments	Disk2\Review\Customer.mdb	
Case Problem 1	Disk3\Cases\MallJobs.mdb	
Case Problem 2	Disk4\Cases\Payments.mdb	
Case Problem 3	Disk5\Cases\Walks.mdb	
Case Problem 4	Disk6\Cases\Lexus.mdb	
Tutorial 2		
Session 2.1	Disk1\Tutorial\Restaurant.mdb *(Continued from Session 1.2)*	
Session 2.2	Disk1\Tutorial\Restaurant.mdb *(Continued from Session 2.1)* Disk1\Tutorial\Valle.mdb	
Review Assignments	Disk2\Review\Barbara.mdb Disk2\Review\Coffee.dbf	Disk2\Review\Valle Products.mdb
Case Problem 1	Disk3\Cases\MallJobs.mdb *(Continued from Tutorial 1)* Disk3\Cases\Openings.mdb	
Case Problem 2	Disk4\Cases\Payments.mdb *(Continued from Tutorial 1)* Disk4\Cases\PlusPays.mdb	
Case Problem 3	Disk5\Cases\Walks.mdb *(Continued from Tutorial 1)* Disk5\Cases\Pledge.db	
Case Problem 4	Disk6\Cases\Lexus.mdb *(Continued from Tutorial 1)* Disk6\Cases\Lopez.xls	
Tutorial 3		
Session 3.1	Disk1\Tutorial\Restaurant.mdb *(Continued from Session 2.2)*	
Session 3.2	Disk1\Tutorial\Restaurant.mdb *(Continued from Session 3.1)*	
Review Assignments	Disk2\Review\Valle Products.mdb *(Continued from Tutorial 2)*	
Case Problem 1	Disk3\Cases\MallJobs.mdb *(Continued from Tutorial 2)*	
Case Problem 2	Disk4\Cases\Payments.mdb *(Continued from Tutorial 2)*	
Case Problem 3	Disk5\Cases\Walks.mdb *(Continued from Tutorial 2)*	
Case Problem 4	Disk6\Cases\Lexus.mdb *(Continued from Tutorial 2)*	
Tutorial 4		
Session 4.1	Disk1\Tutorial\Restaurant.mdb *(Continued from Session 3.2)*	
Session 4.2	Disk1\Tutorial\Restaurant.mdb *(Continued from Session 4.1)* Disk1\Tutorial\ValleCup.bmp	
Review Assignments	Disk2\Review\Valle Products.mdb *(Continued from Tutorial 3)* Disk2\Review\ValleCup.bmp	
Case Problem 1	Disk3\Cases\MallJobs.mdb *(Continued from Tutorial 3)*	
Case Problem 2	Disk4\Cases\Payments.mdb *(Continued from Tutorial 3)* Disk4\Cases\PLUS.bmp	
Case Problem 3	Disk5\Cases\Walks.mdb *(Continued from Tutorial 3)*	
Case Problem 4	Disk6\Cases\Lexus.mdb *(Continued from Tutorial 3)*	